Outlines

Andy Hopkins
Chris Tribble

Series developed by Andy Hopkins and Chris Tribble

Longman

Longman Group UK Limited,
Longman House, Burnt Mill, Harlow,
Essex CM20 2JE, England
and Associated Companies throughout the world.

© Longman Group UK Limited 1989

First published 1989

Set in 9/11 Palatino Roman
Printed in Italy
by G. Canale & C. S.p.A. - Turin

ISBN 0 582 01664 9

Acknowledgements

We are grateful to the following for permission to reproduce
copyright material:

Michael Joseph Ltd for an adapted extract from p 27 *Pears
Cyclopaedia* 93rd edition (pub. Pelham Books); Pressdram Ltd
for simplified vrsions of the articles 'Wham' in *Private Eye* 15/
5/87, 'Operation' in *Private Eye* 27/6/86, 'Baldness' in *Private
Eye* 12/4/87, 'Operation Good Driver' in *Private Eye* 2/8/87 and
'Frog On Pitch' in *Private Eye* 25/12/87.

Thanks also to Alistair Gordon for permission to use extracts
of student writing done by his students at the Bell School of
Languages, Bowthorpe Hall, Norwich, in Unit 3, Writing a
Journal.

We are grateful to the following for permission to reproduce
photographic material in this book:

Associated Press for page 55 (right); Camera Press Limited
(L. Smillie) for page 27; The J. Allan Cash Photo Library for
pages 21 and 23 (bottom left); Barbara Edwards for pages 36
and 38; Tony Gearing of the Independent for page 55 (left);
Susan Griggs Agency Limited for pages 34 and 60; The
Keystone Collection for page 22; Longman Group UK
Limited for page 66; National News Press and Photo Agency
for page 44; Pan Books and Heinemenn Educational Books
1985 for *The State of the Nation* by Stephen Fothergill and Jill
Vincent – a Pluto Project – page 43 (bottom); page 40,
reproduced by kind permission of Pelham Books Limited;
Picturepoint – London for page 23 (top, bottom middle and
bottom right); Private Eye for page 47.

Contents

Map of the book

Unit	Title	Topic	Writing skills	Language focus
1	Improving Your Writing	REFERENCE UNIT	Appropriate style; organisation	Grammar and vocabulary in written English
2	Organising Your Writing Using Linking Words and Phrases	REFERENCE UNIT	Organising writing	Time linkers; coordinating and contrasting conjunctions; pronouns; cohesion
3	Writing a Journal	Student's journals	Structuring writing	Verb forms in describing sequences; justifying; suggesting
4	Writing a Postcard	Holidays – weather, places and incidents	Description; giving brief information	Adjectives of description
5	Writing Small Ads	Finding a flat; finding a companion	Selecting relevant information; ordering of information	Abbreviations
6	Writing a Letter of Thanks	Thanking people	Conventions in formal and informal letters	Politeness
7	Writing Telegrams and Telex Messages	Travel arrangements and business	Reducing messages to a necessary minimum	Articles, auxiliaries and pronouns
8	Writing Short Narratives: A Fable	Traditional tales and folk tales	Paragraph structure in written narratives	Procedural vocabulary in narrative
9	Writing a Report: Describing Graphs	Population changes	Describing statistics and quantative change	Vocabulary in description of change
10	Writing in Newspapers	Reporting unusual incidents	Sequencing information	Participles
11	Writing a Speech	Speeches of introduction	Planning for writing and speaking	Spoken language and written language
12	Writing Narratives: Telling a Story	Thrillers	Organising narrative	Punctuation of dialogue
13	Writing Letters: Expressing Opinions	Public campaigns	Conventions in formal letter writing	Collocation
14	Writing Dialogue	Reporting unusual incidents	Layout for dialogue	Wh- questions
15	Writing Persuasively	Book covers	Matching grammatical forms to writing requirements	Imperatives, modals and adverbs
16	Writing a Composition: Saying What You Think	Diet and health; television	Organising information; stating opinions	Grammar and vocabulary in formal writing

To the teacher

This book aims to develop in learners the ability to write effectively in English for a range of useful purposes. The materials focus on two central areas:

- the organisational conventions of particular text-types (what the 'product' is like)
- the skills a writer needs to approach and see through particular writing tasks (what is involved in the writing 'process')

While **process** and **product** are useful terms for thinking about language use, it seems obvious that good materials should firstly encourage learners to become better writers by focussing on general techniques useful to text creation and evaluation, and secondly provide them with organisational frameworks which make explicit the sociocultural and linguistic conventions that are part of the knowledge base called on by native speakers when they write. This book tries to apply what we know about how people write and how texts are structured in a way which is helpful to learners.

The materials have been designed so that they may be used either in the classroom with a teacher or by students working alone with some monitoring by a teacher. This design feature allows the teacher a great deal of flexibility in organising the balance between what is done as a group in the classroom and what is done by individuals or small groups of students working independently outside the classroom. Suggested answers to all exercises are given in the key at the back of the book.

CONTENT

A detailed list of the book's contents is provided on page 3. However, it is worth pointing out that the first two units differ in purpose and content from the remaining units. Unit 1 is a general awareness-raising unit which requires learners to reflect upon what we understand by 'good' writing. This initial unit is extremely important as it provides a Checklist against which learners are asked to check and improve their first drafts. Each unit refers back to this Checklist. Unit 2 introduces a limited range of linking devices which are of general value to all the writing tasks in the rest of the book.

Each of the remaining units deals with a different text-type. The text types covered in this book are ones that commonly feature in the major international EFL examinations – particularly those set by the Cambridge, RSA and Oxford boards. However, the principal criterion for the selection of text-types is their value to the learner in terms of their usefulness in the real world. Some text-types have been included not because they are often required of a non-native speaker but because they provide a suitable vehicle for focussing on certain process skills.

It is not necessary to work through the book in the order presented. However, you are strongly advised to cover Units 1 and 2 before looking at units in the remainder of the book. This is particularly important if you intend to use the book as part of a self-study scheme.

UNIT METHODOLOGY

In general, the course is structured around a teaching/learning cycle which contains some or all of the following features:

Feature	Purpose
Discussion	• To bring in learners' knowledge • To predict prior to reading activity
Stimulus and Model Text	• To exhibit relation between stimulus and target text-type • To provide model text for analysis – to derive explicit organisational framework
Enabling Activities for Main Writing Task	• To work on information structure and language features • To work on text generation techniques
Main Writing Task (Drafting)	• To go through a process to generate a product similar to the parallel model text
Follow-up 1. Checking and Improving Text using Checklist 2. Comparing Second Draft with Key	• To improve own text • To compare own version with partner's and key text
Extension Activity	• To offer further freer practice

It is important to note that the key is an integral part of each unit. It is not only an 'answer' section but also contains model texts with which the learner is invited to compare his or her efforts at various stages in the unit.

MANAGING THE WRITING CLASS

The writing class provides a number of management problems for the teacher. We have to decide whether or not extended writing will take place *in* the class (the advantage being that we can monitor the process; the disadvantage being that writers work at varying speeds) or *outside* the class (which is administratively preferable but prevents us from being near the learner at the moment that problems actually occur). The following are possible ways of managing the writing class:

	In class	Outside class	In class (Follow-up)
1	Work through whole unit and begin main writing task	Complete main writing task (first draft)	Improve and rewrite
2	Work through unit but do not begin main writing task	Do main writing task	Improve and rewrite
3	Work through unit but do not begin main writing task	Do main writing task Improve and rewrite	Tutorials from time to time to look at first and final drafts

Of course there are many other options for organising the programme. You may wish the learners to work through the unit in a self-study mode and to use the class time as a series of **writing workshops** in which you devote time to individuals and groups working together.

MARKING WRITING

A When to mark and reasons for marking

According to the methodology implied by these materials, the teacher should not see the 'final' written work until it has been drafted, edited, compared with a model, commented on by a peer and rewritten. The purposes of marking at this stage are:

- to encourage and give praise for achievements
- to ensure that the learner has understood and effectively gone through a process of planning, drafting, comparing and rewriting
- to ensure that the learner has got to grips with the objectives of the unit – particularly the organisational conventions of the text-type and its linguistic features

B Establishing a marking code

It is essential that you establish a marking code early on. It is worth writing this down on a sheet of paper and giving a copy to each of the students, who can then utilise it if they wish when editing their own texts.

. When marking a 'final' text try not to cover the page with indiciations of errors. Be positive and point out only those errors which seriously affect communication and which you can say something constructive about.

C Writing Skills profile

A profile sheet is given at the back of the book. You may wish to use this from time to time with the student to give an idea of progress. It is a good idea to complete this with the student in a tutorial session and use it as a basis for discussion. Alternatively, you could ask students to complete it for each other or to use it at intervals to evaluate their own writing.

To the student

This book can be used in the classroom or for self-study. Suggested answers to all the exercises are given in the key at the back of the book. If you are working alone, complete Units 1 and 2 first. When you have done these units you can do the remaining units in whichever order you wish.

After completing the final writing task in each unit you should follow the procedures in the checklist in Unit 1 for improving your writing. Improve and rewrite your text before comparing it with the model in the key. When you have produced your final text, show it to a teacher or if you do not have access to a teacher, to someone who speaks and writes good English. If possible, find a partner to work with and compare and discuss your texts. Remember that the model texts in the key are *suggested* versions. Others are possible. Good luck!

Improving Your Writing

Discussion

1 How do you decide if a piece of writing is successful? There is an obvious minimum standard for things like handwriting or typing, for example, it must be possible to read the writing, but what else are we judging when we read a letter or an essay?

1.1 Work with a partner and think about the five points given below. Then tick (✓) the two points you think are the most important for you when you are assessing a piece of writing. There is no single correct answer here, but some points are much more important than others.

CORRECT GRAMMAR	
APPROPRIATE VOCABULARY	
GOOD SPELLING	
CLEAR ORGANISATION	
CLEAR, APPROPRIATE LAYOUT	

1.2 Below and on the next page you will find two versions of the same letter. Letter B was written first but it is not as effective as it should be. Letter A is an improved version. Read Letter B carefully and compare it with the corrected version.

1.3 Work with a partner and decide what sorts of mistake the writer of Letter B has made; are they mistakes of:

LAYOUT (L)   VOCABULARY (V)
PLANNING (PL)   SPELLING (SP)
STYLE (ST)   PUNCTUATION (P)
GRAMMAR (G)

Some of the places where there are mistakes have been marked with a number. Write the type of mistake in the box at the side of the letter.

Letter A

18, Cambridge St.
Hebden Bridge
Calderdale
W. Yorkshire

December 11th 1988

Dear Mr Reeves,

I am writing to ask if you can help me with a problem.
A few weeks ago I bought a radio-cassette recorder from your shop but yesterday it stopped working properly. When I put the tape in and pressed the 'play' button it simply didn't move. I tried other buttons but unsuccessfully. I thought it must be the tape, so I put another one in but the same thing happened. It was worse than the first time because when I tried to take it out the tape rolled itself round a little wheel inside the recorder.

I would be grateful if you could repair the recorder. I enclose a copy of the guarantee and my receipt.

I look forward to hearing from you soon.

Yours sincerely,
R.C. Samoes.

Letter B

```
¹ December, 11th 1988                                              [1]
                                                                   [2]
                              ² W. Yorkshire
                                18, Cambridge St
                                Hebden Bridge
                                Calderdale

³ Mr Reeves,                                                       [3]
A few weeks ago ⁴ I've bought a radio-cassette recorder but       [4]
yesterday it stopped working properly. When I put the tape
inside it and pressed the 'play' button it simply didn't move. I
tried the other buttons but ⁵ unsucesful. I ⁶ though it must be    [5]    [6]
the tape, so I put another in but the same thing happened. It
was ⁷ worst than the first time ⁸ cos when I tried to             [7]    [8]
⁹ get it back the tape ¹⁰ enrolled itself on a little wheel       [9]    [10]
inside the recorder.

I'm ¹¹ writting to ask if you could ¹² do the necessary            [11]   [12]
repairs on it. I enclose a copy of the guarantee and
my receipt.
¹³ Please fix it.                                                   [13]
                                                                   [14]
                        14 _____
                          R.C. Samoes.
```

Improving Your Writing – A checklist

2 An important way of improving your writing is to have a clear idea of things that you should check before you finish your work. The list given below covers most of the points you should check in a first version of a piece of writing. It is very important and you will be asked to use it in many of the units in this book. It is designed to help you produce clearer, more effective writing.

IMPROVING YOUR WRITING

FIRST CHECK

Check that your writing makes sense
- Is it correctly organised on the page?
  (Writing models in each unit will help you check this.)
- Is the information presented in a clear, logical order?
- Have you put in all the information your reader needs?
- Have you put in unnecessary information?

SECOND CHECK

Check that you have used the right words
- Have you used any words that are too formal or informal?
- Can you replace any of the words in your writing with more precise or more appropriate vocabulary?

Check spelling and punctuation
- Have you made any spelling mistakes?
- Have you punctuated your writing correctly?

Check the grammar

- Have you made any grammatical mistakes?

ESPECIALLY

- Subject/Verb agreement

           s

  (She *live*in Frankfurt.)
- Verb forms

  have been living

  (We *are ~~living~~* here for 5 years.)

  arrives

  (I will meet you when train ~~will arrive~~.)
- Countable and uncountable nouns

  (We need more *information* about this.)
- Correct use of articles

  (They went to ~~the~~ New York)
- Word order

  (I bought a (red) beautiful dress.)

Using the checklist

3.1 Check that the writing makes sense

The following short report is very badly organised. Work with a partner and rearrange it so that it is easier for the reader to understand. The following writing plan will help you.

- History
- Company structure
- Organisation
- Strengths and weaknesses

A. Our production centre is in Wodenswil, the main grain business is in Samstagern and we have big stores in Olten and Au. We also have a small water-mill (although this is not very important for the company) and we have about 200 employees.

B. The only problems that the firm has are that it is rather dependent on the value of the dollar and that sometimes there is too much work to do. At such times our workers are seriously overloaded, but they receive extra payments during these periods and the company continues to do well.

C. Our company makes glue and glucose and is also involved in the grain business. It is 130 years old and has different sections in various parts of the country.

D. The organisation of the company is quite simple. It buys wheat, maize and barley from overseas suppliers and from some local farmers and has eight vans that it uses to deliver glue and glucose to its customers. We don't do a lot of advertising for our products and only advertise in local newspapers.

3.2 Check that you have not used the wrong words

Many of the words in the following pieces of student writing contain words that have been used incorrectly. Work with a partner to improve the text by putting in correct vocabulary for this context. Select words from the list given below.

Describe someone you have seen recently

He opened the door to the library, stepped in and looked towards the tables where <u>persons</u> sat studying and <u>slammed</u> the door carefully behind him.

He was a man of middle height, <u>clothed</u> in a blue coat which looked a bit <u>unmodern</u>, but still <u>went</u> him well. He was in his twenties, had a hard-looking face with dark eyes and thick eyebrows. His hair was brown and short.

As he walked through the library he looked around him as if <u>seeking</u> for somebody. When he <u>glanced</u> the person he was looking for, his severe expression disappeared and was <u>removed</u> by a warm smile.

---

dressed   old-fashioned   people   replaced
searching   shut   noticed   suited

3.3 Check that you have written in an appropriate style

Like the other passages in this unit, the short composition below contains many usage and vocabulary mistakes. The writer has tried to write a formal essay but some of the language is too informal and some of the vocabulary is inappropriate. Work with a partner and use the words and phrases given in the box under the text to replace those that are underlined.

Are factories spoiling our rivers?

Nowadays <u>a lot of</u> factories are very irresponsible. Not only do they use a <u>lot of</u> clean water but they poison the rivers with their chemicals. Moreover, since <u>they haven't cleaned</u> the rivers the water system is <u>getting dirty and dirty</u>. Therefore, we cannot swim and drink any water <u>of</u> the rivers. In addition, <u>we cannot see any</u> fish <u>which can</u> be eaten. As a result fish is very expensive.

There was a <u>matter</u> in Japan a long time ago. A lot of people who ate the fish <u>got</u> ill. This was because the fish had a disease.

In conclusion, we can say it is dangerous to <u>pour</u> filthy water into rivers.

---

a great deal of   became   becoming more and more polluted   dump
many   problem   they have failed to clean   from
fish from the rivers cannot

3.4 Check that spelling, punctuation and grammar are correct

The text below contains many grammar and punctuation mistakes. Work with your partner to improve and rewrite it.

I think one of the best way to learn a language is to stay and life in the country where it is spoken because then have you to speak in every situation in this language, you have to try to make understand so you can get it in a short time. You must study not so long like you must study when you take an evening course every evening in your own country.

Organising Your Writing Using Linking Words and Phrases

1 Put these sentences in the right order to make an amusing story. When you have rearranged the story, think about why you put the sentences in the order you did. What information did you use to help you?

a) The next day, the same thing happened. He ordered a sandwich and a beer again, drank the beer, put the sandwich on his head and left.

b) The man looked confused for a moment. Then he said, 'OK. I'll have a packet of nuts then.'

c) But this time the barman stopped him. 'Look, I've got to ask you this. Why have you got that packet of nuts on your head?'

d) A man walked into a bar and asked for a pint of beer and a sandwich. He drank the beer first, then put the sandwich on his head and left.

e) When the man came in the following day, the barman gave him his beer as usual, but when he asked for a sandwich, said that they had sold out.

f) On the following day the same thing happened. By now the barman was becoming just a little curious, so he decided he would try to find out what was going on.

g) The man looked at him as if he were an idiot. Then he said patiently . . .' I've got these nuts on my head because you didn't have any sandwiches'. Then he left.

h) The barman gave him the nuts. He drank the beer, put the nuts on his head and started to leave.

2 One way we can work out the correct order of the sentences is to use our knowledge of how jokes are organised. However, there are also particular words like *first, next, then,* that also help us to reorganise the sentences. We can call these **time linkers**. Look at the text in exercise 1 again and write down all the time linkers you can find.

3 Read this extract from a letter and insert the time linkers shown below in appropriate places.

then	eventually	as	first of all	later	by	before

> We had a really good New Year. We all went to Wales to visit Diana's long lost relatives in Carmarthen. Her father left there about thirty years ago and lost touch with his brothers and their families, so this was the first big family reunion for a very long time.
>
> [1]_____ we visited two of his nephews where we spent the morning eating and drinking, and [2]_____ we moved on to meet the family of one of his nieces, where we ate and drank some more until early evening. [3]_____ the whole family got together for a party – quite a wild one! I ate and drank so much! [4]_____ one meal finished

another one seemed to begin. ⁵_____ the end of the day I was absolutely exhausted!

We stayed there for three days ⁶_____ driving back. The journey was interrupted a few times because of minor problems with the car and it ended up taking us about ten hours. Anyway, ⁷_____ we got home – just in time to get some sleep before starting work the next morning.

Using the right time linkers

4 Time linkers can be used to link two events. The second event can happen **at the same time as, before** or **after** the first event.

Example:
Same time: *As* I was leaving the shop I met an old friend.
Before: We can't go *until* she comes.
After: Heat some oil in the pan *then* put the meat in.

4.1 Study the sentences a) to e) below and underline the time linkers. Then decide on the order of the events in each sentence. Finally, decide why each linker is used:

- to show two events happen at the same time
- to show an event happens before another event
- to show an event happens after another event

Write each linker in the appropriate column in the grid.

a) Just as I was getting out of my car it started to rain.
b) I met her while I was out shopping.
c) Wait until I come back, and in the meantime think about what you want to do this evening.
d) Fry the onions, then put the meat in and cook it until it's brown. Finally, add the sauce.
e) I hope to have finished by the time the film starts.

SAME	BEFORE	AFTER

4.2 Now use appropriate time linkers to complete these sentences.

a) _____ I was waiting for you I met Jane.
b) You should plan what you want to say _____ you begin to write an essay.
c) _____ you have finished doing an exam you should check your work.
d) _____ I was about to leave the house, the phone rang.
e) If the cassette recorder doesn't work, first check that the switch is on. If it is, _____ open the plug and check the fuse.

Linkers: *and/but* and words that have a similar meaning

Read the text on the right which is taken from a tourist brochure. Put a single line under linkers which are similar in meaning to *and* and a circle round linkers which are similar in meaning to *but*. The first one has been done for you.

Dear John,
I arrived in England last Saturday. I'm living about three kilometres from the school.
Everyone at the school seems very friendly and there are two other French students in my class. The course is good. I feel I have a good chance of passing the exam in June.

Mixed linkers

| after | although | and |
| but | so | because |

5 There are many other words and phrases used to link ideas in speaking and writing. For example, when we want to **add** information we often use *and* to link our ideas. When we want to express reservation or talk about exceptions we often use *but*.

STAY AT HORIZON HOTELS

When you have selected your Horizon Holiday destination why not also choose a Horizon hotel. Although the character and style of the hotels varies from place to place, the same high standards apply everywhere. They offer exceptional value for money and in addition are located conveniently for the beach and local amenities. All the hotels in this brochure are also backed by our guarantee. However, your holiday at a Horizon hotel is likely to run a little more smoothly because we pay attention to the little things that mean so much.

6 Look at this letter from a French student who has just started a course at a language school in Britain. The pieces of text below have been removed from the letter. Decide where to put them, then rewrite the letter.

- although it is only three months away.
- However, I don't speak French with them during the day because we all want to practise our English as much as possible.
- and my course began on Monday.
- and the social programme is quite interesting as well.
- but it only takes me about fifteen minutes to get in every morning by bus.

7 Have you ever suffered from **culture shock**? What do you understand by the words? What sort of feelings did you have? Read the essay extract below. Put appropriate linkers from the list on the left in the gaps.

Culture Shock

I shall never forget my first visit to China. It was completely different from anywhere else I had been. What I remember feeling most was fear. I was in a country about which I knew nothing [1]_____ whose language I couldn't speak. I couldn't read any street signs and I felt lost in the crowds of people that seemed to be everywhere. I had travelled to many different parts of the world before [2]_____ I had never felt so alone and confused. I think I felt fear [3]_____ I was going into the unknown – an unknown culture whose values I did not have any knowledge of. [4]_____ a few days I became a little more accustomed to the sights, sounds and smells of my surroundings [5]_____ I still felt isolated. I talked to a Chinese friend about these things and he said that he had felt the same when he had visited Europe. European food made him ill [6]_____ he didn't eat at all for two days!

Other ways of linking in a text

8 Besides using linking words and phrases, there are other ways in which we make a series of sentences into a text. Look at these sentences. They are grammatically 'correct' as sentences but why do we find them strange as a text?

> The woman gave the boy a small box. The boy took the small box from the woman and put the small box on the ground. The boy opened the small box. Inside the small box was a package. The boy opened the package.

When we write or speak in any language we only say what we *need* to say or write. In the text above we do not need to refer to the woman, the boy or the small box by **name** after the first sentence. We can replace these words by *she, he* and *it*(or by other words).

8.1 Rewrite the text above using *she, he* and *it* where appropriate.

8.2 Study the text below and underline all the words that are used to refer to the people in the story.

> The old lady with the green hat stood up and walked towards the door. George watched her with interest. Then she stopped and turned to face the window. She looked out. A baby was crying in the distance. As she stood there, he noticed a single tear trickle down her cheek. George looked away and the poor woman opened the door and walked out on to the platform.

8.3 We can refer to these different ways of mentioning people, things and events in a text as a **vocabulary chain**. To make texts effective it is important to be able to refer to the same thing in different ways.

Look at the pictures on the left. Picture A shows a young man walking along a road towards an old woman. However, we could see this situation in at least two ways. Look at Picture B. If we think the young man is going to **help** the woman we could refer to them with one set of words. However, if we think he is going to **harm** the woman, we would probably use a different set of words.

a) Work with your partner and make two lists of words to refer to the man and the woman. Look at the examples.

Wants to help the woman:
Man: kind, pleasant,
Woman: elderly, friendly,

Wants to harm the woman:
Man: scruffy, dirty,
Woman: poor, frail,

A

B

b) Read this text written by someone who thought the man wanted to help the woman:

> An elderly woman was standing by the side of the road waiting to cross. A young man of about twenty came along, saw her waiting and smiled pleasantly. He took her arm and offered to help the friendly old woman cross the road. The kind youth noticed that her bag was open and closed it for her.

Now rewrite the text from the point of view of someone who believes the man intends to harm her and steal her money. Use as many of the words you came up with in a) above as you can to refer to the man and the woman.

Writing a Journal

Discussion

1.1 Do you keep a diary/journal? If so, what kinds of things do you write about in it? Do you make notes about appointments and dates? Do you write about your feelings?

1.2 A lot of language learners find it helpful to keep a journal in which they write down what they feel about their lessons and their language learning experiences. They use what they have written as a basis for discussion with their teacher. Do you think this would be useful for you and/or your teacher? Read the extracts below from student journals and decide how they could be helpful to the student (here the writer) and the teacher. The extracts contain some errors but don't worry about them at this stage.

Write your notes here:

> **A:**
>
>
>
> **B:**
>
>
>
> **C:**

Extract A

> Today we did what I always wished to do. We had a test. Tests are important to show you where you still are weak. By a test you feel you are 'strong' or about which topic you need to study more. Why can't we make such an exercise in class? Not as a test but just discuss the problems. Or why not work with such a sheet at home and ask questions at school?

Extract B

> We did a practise in fast reading in the computer room. I like the programm of fast reading. I recogniced that I'm able to read very fast. I think it's because I read a lot. I think my reading speed of an easy book is as high or even higher than my reading speed was in German before I came to England.

Extract C

> When I watch TV I try to listen carefully. The best way to catch a lot is using the video so I can rewind if I didn't understand. I often listen to the same tapes several times so that I understand more and more. It makes me very happy when I suddenly understand the whole meaning of a song. Even in discos, which are quite boring, I enjoy myself listening to the song's words.

Writing task

2 In the journal extracts on page 16 the writers have:

a) described what happened   c) described their feelings

b) given reasons for their feelings   d) made suggestions

Now read the extracts carefully. Find an example of each of the above and underline them.

3 Now study Extract A again and complete the boxes below with the correct number of the section of the text. Look at the example.

1) Today we did what I always wished to do. 2) We had a test. 3) Tests are important to show you where you still are weak. By a test you feel you are 'strong' or about which topic you need to study more. 4) Why can't we make such an exercise in class? Not as a test but just discuss the problems. Or why not work with such a sheet at home and ask questions at school?

| DESCRIBING SOMETHING THAT HAPPENED IN THE CLASSROOM | ☐ |

| MAKING SUGGESTIONS | ☐ |

| DESCRIBING FEELINGS | 1 |

| GIVING REASONS | ☐ |

Language focus

4.1 Describing something that happened in the classroom

a) Underline all the verbs in the sections of the extracts that describe something that happened in the classroom. What tense is used?

b) When we talk about language learning activities we use certain verbs a lot. Decide which verb(s) you can use in the sentences below. Tick (✓) all those that are possible.

	DID	HAD	STUDIED	WATCHED	PRACTISED	
We						a video.
We						a test.
We						answering exam questions.
We						some grammar exercises.
We						a reading passage.

4.2 Describing feelings and giving reasons

a) Look at this sentence. Which of the words underlined do you think describes how this person felt?

> I went to see a film last night but I left early because I was so <u>bored/boring</u>. I couldn't understand anything.

bored here describes the **person's feelings:** I was bored.
boring describes a **quality of the film:** The film was boring.

Look at these words below. Decide which of them can be used to describe your **feelings** and which can be used to describe the **qualities** of a lesson.

	FEELINGS	*QUALITIES*
bored interested exciting excited tired boring dull interesting tiring pleased enthusiastic		

b) When we want to **give reasons** for our feelings, an easy way is to use *because* . . . . Make up reasons to finish these sentences.

i)   I think studying grammar is useful because . . .
ii) I think small groups are better for language learning because . . .
iii) I find it difficult to speak English outside the classroom because . . .

c) Now use these words to write a few sentences which describe something that happened in the classroom, describe your feelings and give reasons.

> Yesterday/interview/people/park./In my opinion/useful/because/speak/ordinary people.

4.3 Making suggestions

When you write a journal that your teacher is going to read it is very valuable and helpful to make suggestions. You can make suggestions in many ways. Here are a few of them:

- I think we should . . .
- I'd like to . . .
- Why don't we . . .

Now try using these beginnings to write three suggestions for the following circumstances:

a) You want to spend more time looking at grammatical problems
b) You want to have regular vocabulary tests
c) You want to do more work on listening skills

Writing task

5 Look at this grid. It includes information that one student decided to put in her journal over four days. The journal entry for the first day is done for you as an example. Write journal entries for the other three days.

	DAY 1	DAY 2	DAY 3	DAY 4
What we did	Watched a video about family life.	Interviewed people in the street.	Wrote an essay.	Had a test.
What I felt	Interesting but difficult.	Interesting but frightening.	Useful for exams but very difficult.	Very useful.
Reasons	Couldn't understand most of it. Too fast.	Embarrassed about speaking. Good to speak to people outside class.	Not enough guidance from the teacher.	Allow you to know your strengths and weaknesses.
Suggestions	Watch short pieces a number of times.	Practise questions before going out.	More guidance from the teacher.	Have a test every week.

DAY 1

Today we watched a video about family life in Britain. It was quite interesting but I found it very difficult and I couldn't understand most of it because the people spoke too quickly for me to follow. I think we should watch the video in short pieces and go back and watch it again until we understand the main points.

Now you write the journal entries for Days 2, 3 and 4.

After writing

6 a) Compare what you have written with your partner's work.
 b) Compare your texts with the key texts on page 73.

Extension activity

7 Try keeping a journal of your English learning experiences. Talk to your teacher about how best to do this. You may want to write *to* your teacher, or you may wish to keep what you have written private – for your eyes only! Don't *only* write in the way suggested in this unit. Other points worth writing about include:

- how you practise your English outside the classroom
- ways of learning English which are useful to you
- your successes and failures related to English language learning

Try to write a little every day. Good luck!

Writing a Postcard

Discussion

1 a) Think of the last time you sent a postcard. Who was it to? Can you remember what you wrote about?

b) Look at the postcards below. Try to decide who is writing to who in each case. Which of them seem strange? Why?

c) Why do people usually write postcards? Who do they usually write them to?

Dear Sir / Madam, Could you please send me further details of the post advertised in the Times on Saturday? Yours faithfully, John Francis (4, Elm Close, Swansea)	Personnel Manager, Metal Box Co., Jersey Marine, Swansea SA18 9TQ	

A

Dear Ms Jones, Your account was overdrawn by £140 at the close of business on Tuesday. Could you please arrange to clear this overdraft as soon as possible. If you are unable to do so, please come in and see me. Mr. R. Rossiter	Pamela Jones, 46, The Heath Stringers Common Guildford England	

B

Dear Jo, Having a lovely time. We're staying in a small hotel on a hill near a tiny secluded beach. Behind us are mountains covered with tall pine trees and sweet-smelling bushes. The weather is fantastic. Hope you're enjoying your holiday. See you when I get back. Miss you. Love, Peter	Jo Thomas 29 Glebe Road NORWICH England	

C

Dear Alfred, Thanks for letting me stay at your flat last week and for the delicious meal. We must get together again soon. All the best, George	Alfred Hinds Flat 4 26, Rhindol Street London NW12 4AW	

D

Dear Tony I'm sorry to have to tell you that we can no longer continue to employ you. I do hope you'll be able to find another job soon. Regards, Ashley	Tony Harper 14 Beale Street, Ipswich IP2 3AQ	

E

Dear Sylvia, I'm writing from a small town in the far north of Saudi Arabia called Al-Ola. Yesterday we met some really friendly people who took us to Madain Saleh, an amazing complex of caves and burial chambers carved out of solid rock. It was a fantastic experience. Driving north tomorrow to the Jordanian border. I'll write again soon. All my love, Keith	Sylvia Jackson The Forge Morely Norfolk NR18 9RF ENGLAND	

F

2 This unit looks at postcards sent by people who are on **holiday** to their friends. Below is a list of some of the things people often write in postcards. Look at postcards C and F in exercise 1. Which of the following can you find in them? Write C and/or F next to each.

a) description of a **place** _____

b) description of the **weather** _____

c) expressions of **feelings** for the person to whom the card is being sent _____

d) arrangements for the **future** _____

e) description of **things that have happened** _____

Language focus

3.1 Describing a place

a) Read the following extract.

> We're staying in a quiet hotel on a hill near a <u>tiny</u> <u>secluded</u> beach. Behind us are mountains covered with tall pine trees and sweet-smelling bushes. Everything is so <u>peaceful</u>.

This extract describes the location and the general atmosphere of the place the person is in. Using a thesaurus and/or a dictionary, write down as many words as you can that could replace the words underlined (they may not mean the same). Write them in the grid at the top of the next page.

SIZE	LOCATION	ATMOSPHERE
tiny **huge**	secluded	peaceful

b) Now look at this picture. Imagine you are staying in the hotel and write a short description similar to that in part a) above

3.2 Describing the weather
Look back at postcard C in exercise 1. What adjective does the writer use to refer to the weather? Now look at these other words that can be used to describe the weather. Put them in the correct place in the grid.

> awful   beautiful   amazing   fantastic   terrible   dreadful
> wonderful   OK   lousy   sunny   hot   freezing   cool
> dull   miserable   quite warm   not too bad   rotten

POSITIVE	NEUTRAL	NEGATIVE
beautiful		**dreadful**

Did you find that some words were difficult to put into the grid? Some words can be positive or negative depending on the circumstances. Which words are they?

3.3 Describing your feelings
It is very common to begin a postcard with a sentence which tells the reader how much you are enjoying yourself. Find an opening sentence that does this in one of the postcards in exercise 1. Write it here.

_____

What do you notice about the structure of this sentence?

3.4 As you can probably see, there is something odd about the sentence. It has no **subject**. It is very common in postcards to leave out the subject if it refers to the **writer**. To include it is a waste of space, and the reader knows perfectly well that it is the writer who is the subject. Look at this text from a postcard. Which words could you leave out if you wanted to?

> Dear John, We're having a lovely time. We went to visit a monastery yesterday - I had to climb 400 steps up the side of a mountain! I look forward to seeing you on my return. Best wishes, Sally.

3.5 Describing something you've done

a) When we describe something we have done we need to make the description interesting to the reader. Look at this dull description of an event and try to make it more interesting.

> We went to see a castle yesterday. It was very nice.

Work with your partner and add information about:

- how you travelled
- what the castle was like
- how you felt

b) Now look at this picture. Imagine you went on a trip in the boat shown in the picture. Write a few sentences to describe what happened. Try to make your description interesting to the reader.

3.6 Closing a postcard

Look at the phrases below. Which of them could you write to a close relative/boy or girlfriend and which to a more distant friend or acquaintance?

CLOSE RELATIVE/ BOY OR GIRL FRIEND	ACQUAINTANCE

Lots of love
All my love
Regards
See you soon
Best wishes
Love
Yours
All the best

Writing model

4 Although it is possible for postcards to be organised in a variety of different ways, it is worth looking at one good model. Rewrite the text on the right so that it fits the model given on the left below.

Dear _____
Describe your feelings
Describe the weather
Describe the place
Describe something you've done
Close

1. See you soon, Harry
2. Dear Jane,
3. Having a wonderful time here in Greece.
4. Our hotel is in a valley about half a mile from the beach.
5. Yesterday we took a boat to Aegina and spent the day lying on the beach and exploring the island.
6. The weather is absolutely wonderful.

Writing task

5 Imagine you are on holiday in the place shown in the picture below. Use the model in exercise 4 to write a postcard to a British friend.

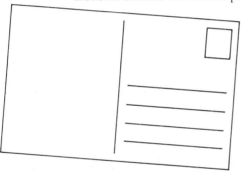 

After writing

6 a) Now try to improve your text by working through the **Improving Your Writing** checklist in Unit 1.
b) Exchange texts with your partner. Compare his/her text with the checklist.
c) Compare your text with the key text on page 74.

Extension activity

7 Choose one of these pictures and write a postcard.

Writing Small Ads

Looking at abbreviations

1 Look at these advertisements taken from a British newspaper. Read them carefully and write the correct number after these sentences.

a) This advertiser wants to sell a child's bicycle. ☐

b) This advertiser wants to find people to share a house with. ☐

c) This advertiser is selling a washing machine. ☐

d) This advertiser wants to meet a female friend. ☐

e) This advertiser is looking for accommodation. ☐

1
PROFESSIONAL PEOPLE
Required to share 3 bedroom house in Edinburgh. Use of all facilities. All mod. cons. Singles – £160 pcm Doubles– £180 pcm incl. Tel. 54736

4
ROOM TO LET
With use of kitchen, bathroom & dining room, no bills. £110 pcm. Tel 518897 office hours only.

7
GAS COOKER
Flavel 70, white – £20. Teak wall unit, good condition – £20. Tel Oxford 505657 day / Eversley 730460 eves.

2
BIKE, girls, suit ages 7 to 10, Raleigh, £25 ono. – Swindon 868949.

5
SPACIOUS SINGLE ROOM
Professional friendly person, for comfy room in lge house in Old Earley. Share all amenities, quiet location, parking. £35 p/w no bills. Tel 766545 eves/ weekends.

8
BUSINESS EXECUTIVE MALE (early 40's) wishes to meet caring and mature lady (up to 45). Please apply to Box No: P562

3
PROFESSIONAL COUPLE SEEKING
furnished/unfurnished accommodation to let in central Brighton for entry in mid June. Tel 470248 between 6–10pm.

6
MOVING SALE, Bendix de luxe washing machine, vgc, £25. – Bradford 690873.

9
PROFESSIONAL PEOPLE
wanted to share house, own room, share kitchen and bathroom, CH, payphone £36pw excl. Tel York 660415 before 8pm.

2 Look at the advertisements again. They contain **abbreviations**. For example *ono* is an abbreviation for *or near offer*. Why do these advertisements often contain abbreviations? Find abbreviations in the advertisements for these words and phrases:

a) per calendar month

b) Telephone

c) per week

d) evenings

e) central heating

f) including

g) excluding

h) modern conveniences

i) very good condition

j) large

3 Now rewrite these advertisements using some of the abbreviations in exercise 2.

a)
For Sale. Amstrad 1640 computer. Very good condition. About £350.

b)
ACCOMMODATION AVAILABLE. Room in large house. £120 per calendar month including all bills. Central heating. Telephone 63421 evenings.

Organisation

4 Good small ads are **short** and **clear**. To save space (you have to pay for every word!) forms of the verb *to be* and words like *a* and *the* are often left out (see the ads in exercise 3). Effective ads usually contain the following:

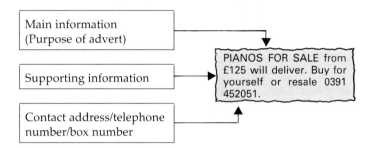

Now put each of these ads in the correct order according to the model shown above. The first one is done for you.

a)
3 Tel. 694612
2 Buyer collects
£10 ono
1 Single bed

b)
Must be easy-going
Professional male
40, cheerful, seeks
female companion
Letter to Box 412

c)
Room wanted near
city centre
Tel. 46312 (eves)
Single male, 25
professional,
non-smoker

Writing task

5 You want to let a small room in your flat. The flat is in Baker Street and your telephone number is 635-7129. You are at work during the day so can only be contacted in the evenings. The room costs £40 per week and has central heating. Fill in this form at the newspaper office. Try to use no more than 13 words in the advertisement. (Abbreviations = 1 word; numbers = 1 word.)

Name: Tel:

Section: (please tick)

| FOR SALE | ACCOMMODATION WANTED | PERSONAL |

| ACCOMMODATION TO LET | EMPLOYMENT |

Write your advertisement here:

Total number of words:
Total cost (20p per word):

6.1 Here are some more small ads. Work with your partner and answer these questions.

a) What sort of ads are they? Are they for accommodation, are they items for sale or are they ads from people looking for friendship?
b) Find an advert from a man under thirty who is interested in sport.
c) Find an advert from a man whose wife has died.
d) Are there any two people who you think should be introduced to each other? Give your reasons.

A CHARMING ATTRACTIVE MALE, slim 35, unattached, well-travelled graduate, own central London flat, responsible job, seeks humorous, healthy, sporty, medium-build, attractive woman under 32 ready for serious relationship. Love of classical music essential. Letter, photo & phone number guarantees reply. Box 4291

B ATTRACTIVE WOMAN graduate, 24 seeks easy-going intelligent caring man for permanent relationship – West/anywhere. Photo appreciated. Box 303.

C SUCCESSFUL attractive career girl, 22 (mad driver), seeks humorous male 23–35 to share love of countryside, dining out and good fun – photo required. Box 2519.

D NEWCASTLE. Male, 29, Cambridge graduate. Humorous and intelligent busy professional seeking similar lady to share interests including theatre, music, sport, walking. Photo please. Box 5879

E PROFESSIONAL WOMAN (36) with daughter (16) seeks companionship with cheerful educated man who enjoys family life. Interest in travel, theatre, music, outdoors added bonus. Preferably Edinburgh, Newcastle, Yorks area. Box 4317.

F VERY ATTRACTIVE successful educated man, 40, kind and generous, seeks liaison amoureux with clean genuine nice young lady London. Need not be rich or glamorous, but photo please. Box 2365.

G EDUCATED WIDOWER 40 living country, kind, reserved, enjoys travel (hot climates), theatre, music, food/wine, laughter, sailing, seeks compatible female. Religion/colour/nationality irrelevant. Write at length in detail with photo(s). Box 6467.

6.2 Organisation

The sequence of descriptions on the left below forms a good model for writing personal ads. Reorder the advertisement on the right so that it matches the model.

Description of advertiser	Photo/phone appreciated Box 9888
Description of person the advertiser is seeking	Warm attractive female. . .
Action/contact address	seeks romantic, unattached, humorous male, 38–50.

Vocabulary development

7 Each of the advertisers uses a lot of adjectives to describe themselves and the people they are seeking. Look at the advertisements in exercise 6 again. Work with your partner and, using a dictionary to help you, find all the adjectives that you think fit into the categories in the grid below.

PERSONALITY	APPEARANCE	EDUCATION/JOB

Writing task

8 Read this text and write an advert for the man. Use the model in exercise 6.2 to help you and make sure you only include information that is **relevant**.

> **"** I'm putting an advertisement in the paper next week. I've just moved to Colchester and I don't really know anyone here yet so I thought it would be a good way to make some friends. I'm not looking for someone to have a close relationship with . . . I just want to find a female friend of about my age who shares my interests and who can help me get to know the town. I'm 25 and I enjoy going out in the evening – to the theatre, to see films, to see live music. I also like playing most sports, but particularly tennis and badminton. I played a lot when I was at university. I'm a teacher now. I'd like anyone who answers the advert to write me a letter before we meet. **"**

Write your advert here. Use no more than 30 words!

After writing

9 a) Work through the **Improving Your Writing** checklist in Unit 1 and try to improve what you have written.
b) Exchange texts with your partner and compare with the checklist.
c) Compare your text with the key text on page 74.

Extension activity

10 Write your own personal advert, describing yourself and the kind of person you'd like to meet. After writing it, collect together all the adverts written by other students and put them up on the wall.
a) Try to identify from the descriptions who the writers of each advertisement are.
b) Try to match up people in the group on the basis of their adverts.

Writing a Letter of Thanks

Discussion

1 We often need to write letters of thanks. Look at the letters below and decide on answers to these questions.

a) What is the relationship between the reader and the writer in each letter?
b) What is the writer thanking for in each letter?
c) Which two letters are most similar? In what ways are they similar?

A

Dear Sir / Madam,

Thank you for your application for the post of 'Temporary Teacher' advertised in The Times last week.

Yours faithfully,

J R Smith
Principal

B

Dear Uncle Tom and Aunty June,

Thank you very much for the radio/alarm clock you sent me for my eighteenth birthday. It's just what I need!
I'm terrible at getting up in the morning and I'm almost always in a bad mood, but now, thanks to your present, I can wake up on time to the sound of music!
I hope you're both well and I look forward to seeing you at Christmas.
Thanks also for the lovely card.
Best wishes,
Peter

C

Dear Jane,

Thanks for putting me up when I was in London last week.
It was great to see you again after so long. I really enjoyed myself.
I hope you can come and stay with me soon.

Love,
Sara

D

Dear Mr Allen,

I am writing to thank you for all the help you gave me during my stay at the school.
As you know, I passed the Cambridge Proficiency exam with a grade B. I know I would never have been able to do it without the encouragement and support I received from your staff.
Please pass on my thanks to Joanna in particular.
I look forward to seeing you all when I visit London in February.
Thank you again for everything.

Yours sincerely,

Roland Maier

2 Letters B and D in exercise 1 are similar in a number of important ways. In both cases, the writer wants to say 'thank you **very much**'; in both cases the **readers** are older and the **writers** go to great lengths to be polite.

> Dear Uncle Tom and Aunty June,
>   Thank you very much for the radio/alarm clock you sent me for my eighteenth birthday. It's just what I need!
>   I'm terrible at getting up in the morning and I'm almost always in a bad mood, but now, thanks to your present, I can wake up on time to the sound of music!
>   I hope you're both well and I look forward to seeing you at Christmas.
>   Thanks also for the lovely card.
>   Best wishes,
>   Peter

Look at this letter again.

a) Underline all the words and phrases the writer uses to express thanks.

b) Try removing paragraphs 2 and 3 completely from the letter on the left. Is it still a good letter?

c) If the purpose of the letter is to express thanks, what are the purposes of paragraphs 2 and 3?

d) Match these descriptions with the paragraphs.

Para 1	Ask about health
Para 2	Say thank you for the first time
Para 3	Say thank you again
Para 4	Explain how the gift will be useful

Language focus

3.1 Writing a first sentence
Look at the first sentence in letter B.

> Thank you very much for the radio/alarm clock you sent me for my eighteenth birthday.

Now write sentences for the following situations:

a) You have been sent some money for your twenty-first birthday.
b) You have been given a book for Christmas.

3.2 Expressing pleasure
We can use a lot of different constructions for expressing pleasure.
a) One way is to say that the gift is nice in some way.

Example:	It's	wonderful
		beautiful
		lovely

Work with your partner and, using your dictionary, write down as many words as you can that can replace *wonderful*.

b) We can also use sentences like these. Can you think of any others?

- It's just what I need!
- It's exactly what I wanted!
- I'm so pleased!
- I'm so grateful!

3.3 Closing a letter

If the letter is to someone who is not a close friend or relative, you should use *Yours sincerely* (if you name the person you are writing to) or *Yours faithfully* (if you address the reader as Dear Sir/Madam).

If the letter is to a friend or relative, close with any of these.

| Best wishes   Love   Best regards   All the best   See you soon |

Writing model

4 Letters of **sincere** thanks usually contain at least two sentences which say *thank you*. As you can see in letter B in exercise 2, these sentences often occur at the **beginning** and **end** of the letter. The remaining paragraphs are included for politeness. A good model for writing a letter of thanks for a gift is as follows.

Your address

Date

Dear _____,

- Say thank you and what you are thanking for. Express pleasure.
- Say how the gift will be useful.
- Ask about health and say you hope to see them soon.
- Say thank you again.
- Close.

Writing task

5 Birgit Hansen lives in Denmark and has just got married. Just before her wedding she received a gift of £100 from the English family she lived with while she was studying in London. She is surprised, pleased and very grateful. This is the letter she wrote. What's wrong with it? Rewrite it to make it more appropriate. Use the model in exercise 4 to help you.

> 77, Vestergade,
> Aarhus
>
> 25 March 1988
>
> Dear Mr + Mrs Abbot,
>
> Thank you for your gift. It's very nice.
>
> Yours faithfully,
>
> Birgit Hansen

After writing

6 a) After writing your first draft, try to improve what you have written by working through the **Improving Your Writing** checklist in Unit 1.
b) Exchange texts with your partner and compare their text with the checklist.
c) Compare what you have written with the key text on page 74.

Extension activities

Either
7.1 You have been on holiday to a farm in Scotland. The farmer and his wife were very kind to you during your stay. Write to them thanking them for their kindness and saying what a wonderful time you had, and how you hope to visit them again some time in the future.

or
7.2 You have recently returned from a period of study at a language school in England. While you were there you lost your bag which contained a large sum of money and a number of important personal possessions. After you left, the bag was found by one of the teachers – a Mr Evans. Write to Mr Evans thanking him for returning the bag. Show how grateful you are!

Writing Telegrams and Telex Messages

Discussion

1.1 A telegram is something that is usually only used in emergencies or when good news needs to be sent quickly and a telephone is not easily available.

Look at the situations below and decide in which ones you might need to use a telegram. If you think it would be very unusual to use a telegram in any of these situations, how would you contact the person in question?

a) You need to borrow some money from your bank, but you do not live near to the branch where you keep your account.   Method:
b) You are in Bogota, the capital of Colombia and you need some money from your parents in France very quickly.   Method:
c) You have missed the train and will be late for work this morning. You want to tell your boss what has happened.   Method:
d) You have been studying in America and you want to tell your parents you have passed an examination.   Method:
e) Your sister in Australia is getting married. You want to congratulate her.   Method:

1.2 Telegrams and telexes are written in similar language but are sent in different ways. Write down what the difference between a telegram and a telex is. Use a dictionary or encyclopedia if you are not sure of the exact difference.

Telegram: _____

Telex: _____

1.3 When are telegrams sent in your country? Work with a partner and find out when and why they think they might send a telegram. Write notes on their answers and find out from other people in your class if they have similar reasons.

_____

_____

Focus on language

2.1 We do not need to write telegrams very often – the telephone has taken over for many purposes. However, there are still situations when it is the best way to get information to another country. For example, the letter below would not be a very sensible way to get urgent information from China to London.

Study the letter and the telegram printed at the top of the next page. Underline the words that have been removed from the letter.

```
                    Tientsin Airport
                    People's Republic of China

                    15.4.88

Janet Evans
Impex Group
17, Great Portland St
London  NW1
UK

Dear Janet,

I have been delayed at the airport and I will not
arrive in London until 17.54 Saturday evening.
Could you please tell Michael what is happening?

Perhaps we could meet at lunchtime on Sunday at my
hotel. The address is:

Hotel Albemarle,
24, Wilton St.
London NW1
(Tel 01-487-5892)

My apologies for the inconvenience.

Yours sincerely,

Katarina Belsdorf
```

```
17.4.88
EVANS. IMPEX GROUP. 17 GREAT PORTLAND ST. LONDON. NW1
DELAYED AIRPORT.   ARRIVE LONDON 17.54 SATURDAY.    PLEASE
TELL MICHAEL.   MEET SUNDAY LUNCHTIME HOTEL ALBERMALE
24 WILTON ST. NW1 TEL 01 487 5892.
KATARINA
```

2.2 What words do you need?

The words that have been removed from the letter can be divided into four main types – **prepositions, personal pronouns, auxiliary verbs, articles**. Write one or two examples from the text of each of these word types.

	EXAMPLES	
PREPOSITIONS		
PERSONAL PRONOUNS		
AUXILIARY VERBS		
ARTICLES		

Model text

3 When you write a telegram it is very important that you put your information in an order that makes your message clear *and only include important information.* Study Katarina's first telegram again and decide where the following section labels should be written.

REQUEST FOR ACTION   INFORMATION

```
17.4.88
EVANS. IMPEX GROUP. 17 GREAT PORTLAND ST. LONDON. NW1

DELAYED AIRPORT.   ARRIVE LONDON 17.54 SATURDAY.   PLEASE
TELL MICHAEL.   MEET SUNDAY LUNCHTIME HOTEL ALBEMALE
24 WILTON ST. NW1 TEL 01 487 5892.

KATARINA
```

Writing task

4 The information in the telegram below is badly organised and contains unnecessary information. Work with a partner to decide on a better way of writing the telegram.

```
16.4.88

BELSDORF. NEW CHINA HOTEL. TIENTSIN. PRC

HAVE TOLD MICHAEL. MY CAR BROKEN DOWN. WILL SEND COMPANY CAR TO
MEET YOU AT AIRPORT. OK MEET SUNDAY. MY FATHER WILL BE COMING
WITH US TOO.  GOOD LUCK FLIGHT. HOPE ALL WELL. BEST WISHES.

JANET
```

Improving your writing

5 Katarina's plane was delayed for another twenty-four hours so she had to send a second telegram to Janet Evans at Impex. The first draft of her telegram is printed below. It contains too many words and needs shortening.

Work with a partner and improve Katarina's telegram. It should be no more than thirty-four words long (including the date).

```
17.4.88
EVANS. IMPEX GROUP. 17 GREAT PORTLAND ST. LONDON. NW1

MY PLANE DELAYED ANOTHER 24 HOURS.  I WILL COME TO LONDON
MONDAY MORNING 6.40 AM.  IS IT POSSIBLE SEND A CAR TO THE
AIRPORT.  PLEASE TELL MICHAEL TO BRING DOCUMENTS TO YOUR
OFFICE.  WE CAN HAVE A MEETING AT IMPEX ON MONDAY AFTERNOON.
PLEASE ACCEPT MY APOLOGIES FOR DELAY.
KATARINA.
```

Writing task

6 Telex messages are now more common than telegrams in many countries and especially in business and government. They are written in a similar way to telegrams.

6.1 Maria Stanisopoulos runs a small import/export business called 'Agrico' in Athens. She received this telex message from her colleague Elizabeth Stevens in London.

```
MED FOODS    LONDON 467312
             ---------------
DATE         15.8.89
             -------

FROM ELIZABETH STEVENS
     -----------------

TO    MARIA STANISOPOULOS
      -------------------

SUBJECT  DELIVERY OF YOGHURT AND OLIVES  (ORDER 3462)
         -------------------------------------------------

PLEASE CONFIRM DELIVERY DATE OF THIS ORDER.  WE EXPECT
LONDON 17.8.89.

IMPORTANT WE RECEIVE SOON.

WITH THANKS
ELIZABETH
```

Mediterranean Foods
– FAX London 498876

Managing Director –
Elizabeth Stevens

6.2 Unfortunately, Maria cannot send the goods to England before the 20th August because of a strike by lorry drivers at the transport company she uses. She has tried to find another company but it is impossible. Her telex to Mediterranean Foods must:

- explain the problem
- apologise
- give the earliest delivery date

Remember to put important information first and only to include things that are relevant.

Agrico	*Athens 39851*
Date	*16.8.89*
From	*Maria Stanisopoulos*
To	*Elizabeth Stevens*
Subject	_____

Improving your writing

7.1 Before you hand in your message, use the **Improving Your Writing** checklist in Unit 1 to help make sure you have written your telex as effectively as possible. (However, note that ordinary grammar rules are not so important in writing telegrams and telexes.) Use the telex message in exercise 6.1 as a key text.

7.2 Get a partner to check your work to see that there is no unnecessary information and that you have written your message as clearly and simply as possible. Then check your writing with the key text on page 75.

Extension activities

Either

8.1 You are on holiday in Indonesia and you have lost all your luggage. You have enough money to send a telegram of no more than thirty words (including the address) to your aunt who lives in Manchester, England. Write a telegram that explains your problem and asks her to send you enough money to buy an airline ticket home.

You are staying c/o YMCA, Jakarta, Indonesia. Your aunt's name and address is:

Ms Emily Price
16, Kings Road
Manchester
UK

Use the telegram in exercise 3 as a key text.

or

8.2 Work in a group and invent a small company. Decide what things you make or sell and where you are located. Write a telex to a supplier asking them how quickly they can provide things that you need for your business. Write a second telex giving their reply.

Writing Short Narratives: A Fable

Discussion

1 Every language and culture has stories that are told to children to entertain and teach. What stories can you remember? Tell your partner a story that you remember from when you were young. It can be a fairy story or any other kind of tale, but it should have some sort of **moral** to it, that is, a message that teaches something about life.

As you listen to your partner's story, write notes under the following headings. When they have finished their story you should tell them yours.

SETTING	WHO	EVENTS
		• • • • • • •

MORAL

You will use these notes when you are writing a story at the end of this unit.

Aesop's Fables

Aesop's Fables are a collection of stories written nearly 2500 years ago in Ancient Greece. Each story is quite short but it has some sort of moral or lesson in it. This unit will look at how you can write short stories like this.

Preparing for writing

2 The story below has been printed in the wrong order. Read it carefully and decide on the correct order for the different sections. Write the correct number for each paragraph in the boxes beside the text.

The Fox and the Crow

The fox came and sat under the tree and looked up at her and said, 'What a beautiful bird I see above me. She has the blackest, brightest feathers in all the world and the sharpest, shiniest beak I have ever seen. If her voice is as sweet as her looks she must be the Queen of all the birds.' ☐

It was an ugly, harsh caw! Down came the cheese and, of course, the fox caught it before it touched the ground and ran off, saying, 'I see you have a voice, madam, it's a pity you don't have brains as well!' ☐

The crow was a very vain bird and wanted to show the fox how well she could sing. She forgot about her cheese ☐

> and opened her sharp, shining beak to sing the only note she knew.
>
>   A crow was sitting on the branch of a tree with a piece of cheese in her mouth when a hungry fox saw her and started to think of how he could get the cheese for himself.

☐

2.1 Discuss your reasons for putting the sections in the order you chose. Do you agree with one another? Use the following section labels as a way of helping explain your decision. Which section number matches the labels?

	LATER EVENTS		EARLIER EVENTS
	SETTING THE SCENE		DESCRIBING THE FINAL OUTCOME

When you have to write any sort of narrative, this is a very common way of organising your ideas.

2.2 Language focus

Traditional stories usually have very clear sections at the beginning in which the scene is set. 'Once upon a time . . .' is the way hundreds of English fairy tales begin.

Study these examples from Aesop's Fables and underline the words that do the same job as 'Once upon a time'.

a) One day, a Hare was making fun of a Tortoise . . .
b) Once there was a farmer who was working on his farm when . . .
c) Long ago there was a king who loved gold . . .
d) There was a time when all the animals could talk. . .

2.3 Pronouns

Study the words that have been underlined. The writer uses many different **pronouns** to refer to the crow.

> The fox came and sat under the tree and looked up at <u>her</u> and said, 'What a beautiful bird I see above me. <u>She</u> has the blackest, brightest feathers in all the world and the sharpest, shiniest beak I have ever seen. If <u>her</u> voice is as sweet as <u>her</u> looks <u>she</u> must be the Queen of all the birds.'

Underline the pronouns that have been used for the fox and the crow in the passage below.

> A crow was sitting on the branch of a tree with a piece of cheese in her mouth when a hungry fox saw her and started to think of how he could get the cheese for himself.

3 The next story is also from Aesop's Fables. The version that is printed here is a first draft of the writing and needs revising before it is finished. The story should contain four paragraphs, there are two places where there are some words missing and also there are many mistakes in the prepositions that have been used.

Work with a partner to rewrite the story into four paragraphs that follow the same pattern as the story of the Fox and the Crow and add the correct prepositions and missing words.

The Sun and the North Wind

_____ the Sun and the North Wind had an argument over who was the strongest. The North Wind said, 'I am stronger than anything. I can blow <u>up</u> the tallest tree and take the roofs <u>of</u> all the houses!' In order to discover the truth they agreed to test their strength <u>at</u> a traveller. They would see who would be the first to take his coat <u>out of</u> his back. The North Wind was the first to try. He gathered all his force and began to blow as hard as he could. However, the harder the wind blew, the tighter the man held on to his coat, so that in the end the North Wind was so exhausted he had to give up. _____ the Sun began, all he had to do was to shine brighter <u>for</u> the sky. At first the man undid the buttons of his coat. Then, as the sun's warmth increased, the man took <u>out</u> his coat and carried it over his arm. He was very happy to walk along like this, feeling pleased <u>from</u> the change <u>with</u> the weather. The North Wind was very angry and went off behind the hills, but the Sun rose higher and higher <u>to</u> the sky. 'Don't you know that persuasion is better than force!' he said.

4 The next story is about a shepherd boy and a wolf.

4.1 Before you write the story you will need to decide on the correct labels for the pictures at the top of page 39. Write the appropriate number beside each picture.

The Boy Who Cried 'Wolf!'

1. a boy looked after sheep
2. many sheep were killed by the wolf
3. one day a wolf really came to attack the sheep
4. he did this several times and the villagers were angry with him
5. he frightened people in his village by saying a wolf was attacking the sheep
6. he ran to tell the villagers but they did not believe him

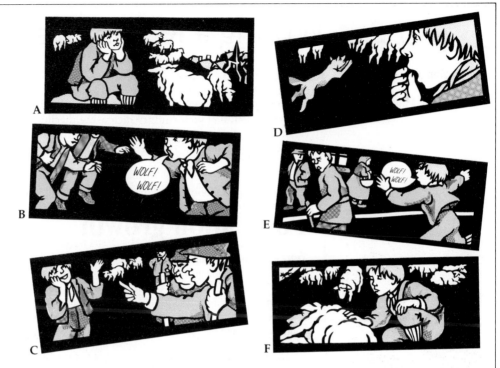

4.2 Now write the story of **The Boy Who Cried 'Wolf!'**. Remember to use appropriate punctuation for speech and to organise your story into sections which:

- set the scene
- describe earlier events
- describe later events
- describe final outcome

The vocabulary below will help you write your story. Try and use as many of these words as you can.

> looked after   sheep   joke   frighten   pretending   attack   shout   fields
> laughed   several times   help   tricks   really   loudly   go away
> believe   tricks   lies   killed   beaten   believe   liar   truth

Improving your writing

5.1 When you have finished your story use the **Improving Your Writing** checklist in Unit 1 to help make sure that you have organised it appropriately and that you have not made any serious mistakes in grammar, spelling or punctuation.

5.2 Compare your work with the key text on page 76 and check that you have covered the different sections that the story needed. Once you have understood the differences between your story and the key text make any changes and corrections that you think are important to your own piece of writing.

Extension activities

6 a) Use the notes that you made in Section 1 to help you write a story, of the same sort of length as the ones in this unit. You may need to ask your partner for extra information, but your notes should be enough. Use the same writing pattern as the one you have studied in this unit.

b) When you have finished your writing and checked it carefully, exchange stories with other members of your class and see whose story you like most. The stories can be funny or sad, they can have a lesson in them or can just be told to entertain.

Writing a Report: Describing Graphs

Discussion: Population

1 Work with your partner and decide on answers to the following.
a) Is the population of your country increasing, declining or static?
b) What factors do you think affect population growth?
c) Should governments try to control population growth? If so, how can they do it?

Reading

2 Read this passage about population growth and fill in the notes below.

Population growth

Years of studies, warnings and forecasts by population analysts of the risks to mankind of continuing population growth have, at last, begun to have some effect. Although the actual numbers of people in different countries are not declining, the rate of growth is.

A number of factors affect population growth. These include, among others, the level
5   of medical care available, the availability of food, attitudes to family size, attitudes to contraception, and the rate of death amongst children and adults.

United Nations agencies have concluded that programmes for reducing population growth should aim to: reduce child mortality by making better medical care available; make family planning information and services accessible; encourage the idea of small
10 families. Although reducing child mortality will initially cause an *increase* in population, it is felt that in the long term, families will have fewer children because parents will have more confidence that their children will survive.

Factors affecting population growth:	**Aims of population control programmes:**
•	•
•	•
•	•
•	
•	

3 Now study the graph and read the text at the top of the next page. Part of the graph is missing.

Draw in the missing part from information in the text.

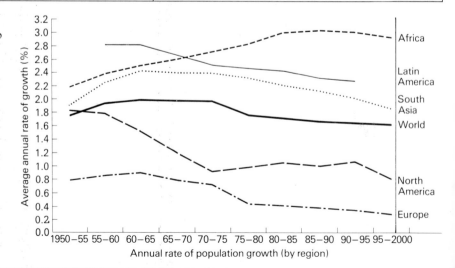

Annual rate of population growth (by region)

During the period covered by the graph, the rate of population growth for the world has declined very slightly, from 1.8% in the early 1950s to about 1.7% in the 1980s. However, during the sixties and early seventies, this figure reached a peak of almost 2%. The projected global figure for 2000 is 1.6%.

5   In terms of reducing the rate of population growth, Latin America has had a great deal of success. From a figure of around 2.7% in 1950, the rate reached a peak of 2.8% in the early sixties, then fell dramatically to approximately 2.5% in the seventies. It is hoped that the rate will continue to fall, reaching 2.2% by the year 2000.

    The rate of population growth in North America has also dropped significantly

10 over the period. Starting at around 1.8% in the fifties the rate plummeted to about 0.9% in the early seventies. However, the seventies saw a gradual rise back to approximately 1% by the early eighties. By 2000 the rate is expected to reach a record low of 0.8%.

Organisation

4.1 Text organisation

The text in exercise 3 has three paragraphs. Decide which of the following descriptions matches each paragraph. Draw lines between the paragraph and the description.

Paragraph 1   Details of the changes in a particular region
Paragraph 2   The overall picture of world population growth
Paragraph 3   Details of the changes in a particular region

4.2 Paragraph organisation

All three paragraphs in the text in exercise 3 are organised in a similar way. Draw lines between the sentence and the description so that the sentences are in the order they occur in each of the paragraphs.

Sentence 1   Expectations for the future
Sentence 2   General comment on whole period for a named area
Sentence 3   Details of changes during each time period

4.3 Organising texts and paragraphs: from GENERAL to PARTICULAR

If you completed exercise 4.2 correctly you will have noticed that each of the paragraphs in the text in exercise 3 begins with a **general** point then moves on to a **particular** point.

- The text starts with the world figures (**general**) before introducing figures for each region (**particular**).
- The paragraphs start with a comment on the changes during the whole period covered by the statistics (**general**) then give details of changes for each period (**particular**).

Look at these pairs of sentences. Mark them either general (G) or particular (P).

a) Europe is suffering from the effects of industrial pollution. ☐

b) In Norway the trees are dying. ☐

c) I spent two hours waiting to see a doctor yesterday. ☐

d) Medical services in Britain are getting worse. ☐

e) The divorce rate has increased dramatically. ☐

f) Patterns of family life are changing. ☐

Language focus

5.1 Describing changes (1)
Look at this sentence.

> . . . the rate of population growth for the world has **declined** very slightly . . .

a) Underline all the **verbs** used in the text in exercise 3 that the writer uses to describe changes in the population growth rate.
b) Here is a longer list of verbs that can be used to describe changes in statistics over a period of time. Using your dictionary/thesaurus, decide whether they indicate an **upward** (U) or **downward** (D) movement.

increase ☐   decrease ☐   rise ☐   grow ☐   plummet ☐
decline ☐   soar ☐   drop ☐   leap ☐   slump ☐
dive ☐   rocket ☐   shoot up ☐

5.2 Describing changes (2)
We can also use **adjectives** and **adverbs** to describe degrees of change in statistics. Look at these sentences.

> There was a **dramatic** rise . . . (adjective)
> The rate increased **dramatically** . . . (adverb)

a) Underline all the adjectives and adverbs in the text in exercise 3 that indicate change.
b) Rewrite the sentences below as shown in the example.

Example: There was a dramatic rise in the population growth rate.
  The population growth rate rose dramatically.

i)   There was a sharp increase in the rate in the 1960s.

_____

ii) There was a slight fall in the rate in the 1970s.

_____

iii) There was a sudden leap in the rate in 1940.

_____

c) Here is a list of adjectives that can be used to describe change. Using a dictionary/thesaurus, decide whether they indicate a **small** (S) or a **large** (L) change.

gradual ____ sudden ____ rapid ____ steady ____
great ____ slight ____ dramatic ____ moderate ____

Now write an appropriate adjective in the gaps on the right to describe the changes in this graph. One is done for you as an example.

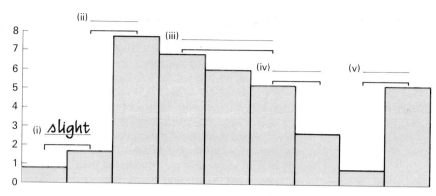

(i) _slight_

Writing task

6 Look at the graph and text in exercise 3 again. Write two paragraphs using information from the graph, one about Africa and the other about Europe. Use the models you looked at in exercise 4 to guide you.

After writing

7 a) Try to improve your writing by working through the **Improving Your Writing** checklist in Unit 1.
   b) Exchange texts with your partner and compare his/her text with the checklist.
   c) Compare your text with the key text on page 76.

Extension activity

8 Here is another kind of graph. It shows how the population of Britain changed between 1901 and 1980. Write a short report describing the changes. Make particular comparisons between the following:

a) the general shape of each graph
b) the percentage of children under 5 in 1901 compared with 1980
c) the percentage of people aged 30–34 and 60–65 in 1980 compared with 1901 (Can you think of any reasons for the 'baby boom' that happened in the late 1940s and around 1920?)
d) the ratio of women to men over 70 in 1980 compared with 1901

MORE OLD PEOPLE

Age of the population millions

Age	1901		1980	
85 and over	0.02	0.04	0.14	0.43
80-84	0.06	0.09	0.27	0.66
75-79	0.13	0.18	0.60	1.06
70-74	0.23	0.30	0.98	1.40
65-69	0.33	0.41	1.27	1.58
60-64	0.49	0.58	1.32	1.50
55-59	0.58	0.65	1.63	1.74
50-54	0.75	0.82	1.57	1.62
45-49	0.89	0.95	1.56	1.55
40-44	1.05	1.12	1.63	1.59
35-39	1.20	1.29	1.73	1.70
30-34	1.35	1.48	2.07	2.05
25-29	1.56	1.75	1.94	1.87
20-24	1.73	1.94	2.14	2.03
15-19	1.90	1.93	2.38	2.26
10-14	1.97	1.96	2.30	2.19
5-9	2.05	2.05	2.02	1.91
under 5	2.19	2.19	1.75	1.66

Writing in Newspapers

The British magazine *Private Eye* has published a regular feature called 'True Stories' for many years. It contains short articles taken from newspapers from different English speaking countries. These articles are always either very strange or very funny. In this unit we shall look at the way this sort of short article is written and you will be writing your own 'True Stories'.

Discussion

1.1 Work in groups of three or four. This picture was used to illustrate a newspaper article. What do you think the article was about? Make some notes of your ideas and use them to tell your version of the story to your group. Compare the stories that your group invented with another group's. Who made up the best story?

1.2 Have any people in your class heard any stories recently from newspapers, radio or television that have been strange or amusing? Tell your class about the story, where you heard or read it and why you thought it was interesting.

Preparing for writing

2 Journalists often write in very similar ways, even if they are writing for different newspapers.

- First they introduce the most important person or people in the story.
- Then they write about the main event or events.
- Finally they describe the outcome of these events.

2.1 Organisation
Read the two short newspaper articles below and decide where each of the sections above begins. Write down the first five words of each section.

Model text 1

Trapped under his car for six hours, Mr Gordon Pickrell of Kingston told the police: 'I broke my arm when the car turned over in the accident and it was balanced just above my shoulders and neck. I was in a great deal of pain and very frightened.

'However, the cause of my attack on the rescue team was not the pain. It was having to listen to a cassette of the rock group WHAM! playing over and over again throughout the entire period. At first they made me think I was going mad, then I thought I was going to die. Then I wanted to die.

'That was why I hit the ambulance man when I was finally released.'

Model text 2

Asked why he had decided to leave the hospital a few moments before was his operation was due to start, Mr Kevin Heatherton said: 'I was lying down waiting for the anaesthetic when two surgeons began to argue about who was going to do the work. Seconds later one hit the other with his fist and they started to fight.

'As they struggled with each other on the floor of the operating theatre I slipped away.'

1._____   1._____

2._____   2._____

3._____   3._____

2.2 What do you think would be the best titles for these articles. Choose one of the following or write your own titles.

- Insult to Injury
- A Narrow Escape
- Theatre Drama
- Rescuers Assaulted
- Dangerous Doctors

Article 1:_____ Article 2:_____

2.3 Grammar

In this sort of very short article it is important to say things as briefly as possible. Journalists often use participles as a way of using as few words as possible and also as a way of helping put important information at the *beginning* of their story.

Compare the two different versions of the opening sections of the two articles that are given below.

Trapped under his car for six hours, Mr Gordon Pickrell of Kingston told the police:

Mr Gordon Pickrell of Kingston, the man who was trapped under his car for six hours, told the police:

Asked why he had decided to leave the hospital a few moments before his operation was due to start, Mr Kevin Heatherton said:

Mr Kevin Heatherton was asked why he had decided to leave the hospital a few minutes before his operation was due to start. Mr Heatherton said:

In both of these articles the **event** is more important than the name of the person. Using participles can be a very effective way of putting important information at the beginning of an article.

Writing task

3 Both of these extracts below could be the beginnings of short newspaper articles, but they are not written in an appropriate style. Work with a partner to rewrite the extracts so that they could make more appropriate beginnings for newspaper articles.

Article 3

Mrs Shano Urati of Tokyo, was interviewed at her mother's house. She said:

_____

_____

Article 4

Mr John Topton, a counter clerk at Barclay's Bank, Snairwell, was interviewed outside his place of work. He said:

_____

_____

Writing task

4 Work with a partner to put the rest of Article 3 into the right order. Remember that the article will need a surprising or interesting ending.

After accepting this advice he ate nothing for 40 days and on the 41st he died.

His hair had shown no signs of re-turning.

A street-doctor convinced him that the only certain way to cure his bald-ness was to fast.

My husband worried about losing his hair.

(*Private Eye*, 16th October, 1987)

Improving your writing

5 The rest of Article 4 contains several mistakes and needs to be rewritten. Working with a partner, rewrite the article so that it presents the information clearly and contains no grammar, spelling or punctuation mistakes.

Mr John Topton, a counter clerk at Barclay's Bank, Snairwell, was interviewed outside his place of work. He said:
'We was busy at lunchtime and there was a long cue. All at once a man came under the rail, stuck a gun over the counter and demand the money in my cash drawer. I was about to followed the manager in-structions for hand over some moneys and press the alarm's bell, when Mr Bobby Grove, a customer who is waiting to be served, and came up behind the man, grabbing him and, shouting, "Queue jum-per!", marching him out of the bank and into the street. It was quiet the relief.'

Writing task

6.1 Use the notes given below to write a short newspaper article about an incident that took place in France. Begin your article like this: 'Reporting on the results of Operation Good Driving . . .'

Country: France
Person involved: Minister of Transport Monsieur Pierre Mehaingerie

Situation: Police wanted give cash prize good drivers. BUT could not find any.

1. Motorway patrols search. Found one good driver but he suddenly went fast (140 kph) – disappeared into thick traffic. No one wearing seat-belt or within speed limit.
2. 2nd good driver went past 3 red lights (no good reason).

Action: No prizes – driver through red lights must pay large fine.

6.2 When you have written your article, check it against the model texts you have studied in this unit and then use the **Improving Your Writing** checklist in Unit 1 in order to make sure that your writing is written in the appropriate style and that it contains no mistakes.

6.3 When you have checked your work, rewrite it carefully before comparing it with the key text on page 76.

Extension activities

Either

7.1 Make a collection of articles from newspapers or stories that are broadcast on television or radio and write your own 'True Stories' page for a class newspaper.

or

7.2 Write a short newspaper article based on the cartoon below. It is about something that is not a true story at all! However, if something like this did happen, the newspapers would certainly write about it.

The lady in this picture is called Susan Sharples and she lives in a small house in the suburbs of Barnsley in Yorkshire.

*"George can you come home?
The tortoise is in one of his moods"*

Write about the dreadful afternoon when her tortoise destroyed their living room. Begin your article like this:

'Interviewed in the front room of her . . .

Writing a Speech

Certain international examinations of English language require you to write a short speech. This unit gives advice about and practice in producing a **written** speech of this kind.

Discussion

1 a) Have you ever had to make a short speech in your own language? What was the occasion? Did you do it well? Did you speak from notes or did you read word for word something you had written?

   b) Imagine this situation. A student at a college in Britain has been asked to introduce a guest speaker who is coming to give a talk. The speaker is a diplomat who will be talking generally about some aspects of diplomacy, and will be making reference to the role of diplomats in dealing with international incidents – in particular, hijacking. The talk will be open to students, staff and guests. He is trying to think of what to say.

   Tick (✓) those things in the list below that you think he should include his introduction.

- welcome the guests ☐
- refer to her salary ☐
- give details of her career and experience ☐
- welcome and express gratitude to the speaker ☐
- refer to her home life ☐
- refer to the length of the talk ☐
- introduce the speaker by name and refer to the general subject of the talk ☐
- introduce the particular topic and relate her experience to it ☐
- wish her good luck for the future ☐
- propose a toast* ☐

> * *toast*: when you ask people to drink to someone's health and good fortune

2 The student has decided on a list of points to include in his speech. Here are his notes. Now compare them with the following speech and see if they are in the correct order. If not, reorder them by writing numbers 1 to 6 in the boxes.

Dr Tomlinson's Talk
- Welcome guests ☐
- Thank Dr Tomlinson for coming ☐
- Refer to length of talk + questions ☐
- Introduce hijacking + her experience in this area ☐
- Refer to her career ☐
- Introduce Dr Tomlinson + general topic of talk ☐

> Good evening ladies and gentlemen. Thank you for coming. It gives me
> great pleasure to introduce our guest speaker for this evening, Dr Claire
> Tomlinson, who is going to address us on the subject of international
> diplomacy – a topic she knows a great deal about.
> 5   Dr Tomlinson began her highly sucessful career as a diplomat working
> at the British Embassy in Rabat, Morocco, where she worked in the
> Cultural Section until 1975. She then took up the post of First Secretary at
> the Embassy in Cairo and remained in Egypt for eight years. In 1983, she
> moved to Amman where she became the first
> 10 woman ambassador to Jordan, the post which she currently occupies.
>   Dr Tomlinson is an expert in Middle East affairs, and a particular
> interest of hers is the highly topical issue of hijacking. She has been
> directly involved in the delicate discussions that take place between
> governments over international incidents of this kind, and her talk will
> 15 concentrate on the role of diplomats in resolving such crises.
>   May I take this opportunity of thanking you, Dr Tomlinson, for giving
> up your valuable time to be here with us this evening and for agreeing to
> give us the benefit of your long experience.
>   I understand Dr Tomlinson is going to speak for about one hour,
> 20 and will leave about half an hour for questions and comments. So, would
> you please welcome tonight's speaker, Dr Claire Tomlinson.

Language focus

3.1 Saying complimentary things about a speaker

The main purpose of an introduction to a guest speaker is to make the audience
interested in what the speaker is going to say. The introduction should
emphasise:

- the importance and value of the speaker
- the relevance of her/his experience to the topic

Read the whole text in exercise 2 again and underline all the parts of the speech
which indicate to the audience that the speaker is worth listening to.

Introducing a speaker

3.2 One aspect of politeness in an introductory speech involves **expressing
pleasure** that the speaker has agreed to come.

a) Look at this:

> It gives me great pleasure to introduce our guest speaker for this
> evening, Dr Clare Tomlinson, who is going to address us on the
> subject of international diplomacy – a topic she knows a great deal
> about.

Instead of: 'It gives me great pleasure to . . .' we could say:

I am *pleased/happy* to introduce . . .

Work with your partner and, using a dictionary/thesaurus to help you, decide on
other words that could replace those in italics.

b) Another aspect of politeness is to say that the speaker is knowledgeable about
the subject. Instead of 'a topic she knows a great deal about' we could say:

a topic she is very familiar with . . .
an area in which she is an acknowledged expert . . .

Can you think of any other ways of saying the same thing?

c) Look at this introduction. It includes no compliments and is therefore quite impolite. Rewrite it to include compliments.

> This is Mr Clark who is going to talk to us about international finance.

Describing someone's career and experience and relating it to the topic

4 Look again at these two paragraphs from the speech.

> Dr Tomlinson began her highly successful career as a diplomat working at the British Embassy in Rabat, Morrocco, where she worked in the Cultural Section until 1975. She then took up the post of First Secretary at the Embassy in Cairo and remained in Egypt for eight years. In 1983, she moved to Amman where she became the first woman ambassador to Jordan, the post which she currently occupies.
>   Dr Tomlinson is an expert in Middle East affairs, and a particular interest of hers is the highly topical issue of hijacking. She has been directly involved in the delicate discussions that take place between governments over international incidents of this kind, and her talk will concentrate on the role of diplomats in resolving such crises.

4.1 Looking at verb forms
a) Underline all the verbs in the two paragraphs in exercise 4 above.
b) Now list the verbs under these headings:

Verbs that refer to a particular time in the past	Verbs that refer to the past, but not to a particular time	Verbs that describe her qualities and interests	Verbs that refer to the coming talk

4.2 You can see that the first paragraph above contains verbs in the **simple past** which describe events in Dr Tomlinson's career. The second paragraph looks at this past career in relation to the present qualities which she brings to the talk. The **present perfect** (*has been directly involved in . . . .*) links the past with the present. This can be represented like this:

SIMPLE PAST	*PRESENT PERFECT*	*SIMPLE PRESENT*
To describe events in her past	To link these past events to present qualities	To describe her qualities

Writing task

5 Now look at these notes about another speaker and write two paragraphs similar to those in exercise 4 above which describe the person's career and relate it to the topic of the talk.

Name:	**Topic:**
Mr John Clark	The role of international lending agencies in funding agricultural projects.

> **Career details:**
> 1973 – Started career/Bank of England International Section
> 1977 – Became youngest ever director of large merchant bank
> 1983 – Joined World Bank
> 1987 – Became Vice-President of World Bank
>
> **Qualities:**
> * expert on funding of international projects
> * involved in irrigation projects in Sri Lanka, China and Egypt

Writing task

6 The notes on the left below have been provided by a speaker who is coming to give a talk at a college. The person introducing the talk studied the notes and then wrote the speech below. It is full of all kinds of mistakes. Work with your partner and try to improve it. Use this model to help you.

Paragraph 1 Welcome the guests and introduce the speaker and the topic
Paragraph 2 Give details of her career
Paragraph 3 Relate her career and experience to the topic of the talk
Paragraph 4 Thank her for coming
Paragraph 5 Refer to the length of the talk and ask the audience to welcome the speaker

> Name: Ms Yvonne George MP
> Topic: Care of the mentally disabled
> Career:
>   1974 – Joined Camden Social Services as social worker
>   1979 – Became MP
>   1985 – Became Minister of Health and Social Security
> Qualities/Experience
> • concerned with care of the mentally disabled
> • involved in schemes to integrate mentally disabled into the community
> Length of talk: 45 minutes
>   with 15 minutes for questions

Hello everybody. I want to introduce the speaker Yvonne George who is speaking about the care of mentally disabled. Yvonne began her career in 1974. She join Camden Social Services to be social worker. Then in 1979 she become Member of Parliament, and at 1985 the Minister of Health and Social Security.
Miss George know well the mentally disable problem and have been involve in schemes to integrate them in the community.
Thank you Mrs George for to come here tonight.

After writing

7 a) Work with the **Improving Your Writing** checklist in Unit 1 and try to improve what you have written.
b) Exchange texts with your partner and compare his/her writing with the checklist.
c) Check your text against the key text on page 77.

Extension activities

Either
8.1 Is there anyone well-known that you would enjoy listening to? Imagine a famous person is coming to your school to give a talk and you have to introduce them. Perhaps you'd like to hear Mr Gorbachev, Ronald Reagan, Ayotollah Khomeini, Michael Jackson, Diego Maradonna? Find out some details about their careers and imagine a suitable topic for a talk. Then write a short speech introducing them to your classmates.

or
8.2 Use the notes in exercise 6 above to find out about your teacher or a fellow student. Write an introductory speech for him/her.

or
8.3 Invite a real speaker and compose a real introduction!

Writing Narratives: Telling a Story

1 A **narrative** usually describes a sequence of events which took place **in the past**. This unit looks at narrative in relation to telling stories.

Read the story below. While you are reading, think about these questions, then discuss them with your group.

a) Has the woman been in the room before?
b) Is the woman surprised to find someone in the wardrobe?
c) What do you think the relationship is between the man and the woman?
d) What do you think has happened before this episode?
e) What do you think will happen next?
f) From whose point of view is the story told? Through whose eyes do we see the room?
g) Now give the text a title.

> I moved silently up the stairs towards the door. I turned the handle slowly. The door was not locked. It opened noiselessly and I peered in. The room was small and airless with a layer of dust covering the bare floorboards.
>
> 5 I entered and closed the door behind me. There were a few pieces of old furniture in the room – a table with two broken chairs and a dirty sofa stood each side of the window and a large wooden wardrobe stood in the corner. Everything was quiet.
>
> I crossed the room to the window and looked out. The street was empty. I turned to face the room again, and as I did, I thought I
> 10 heard a scraping sound. I could feel that I was getting close now. I walked towards the wardrobe trying to move as quietly as possible. As I reached for the handle my hands began to tremble . . . I pulled suddenly at the door . . . and there he was . . .

2 a) The action in the text above is presented in the order it happened. Look at the diagram of the room below and draw lines to show how the woman moved around the room. Put numbers 1, 2, 3, 4 to show where she stopped.

b) Now compare the points on the diagram where the woman stopped with the paragraph structure of the story. What do you notice?

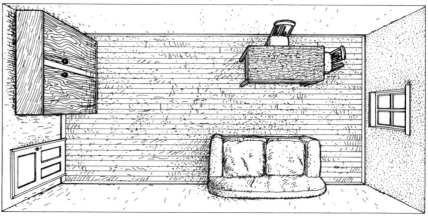

Vocabulary development

3.1 a) Study the text again and write down all the words the writer uses to tell the reader about **sounds**.

silently, _____

b) The writer tells us that the woman 'moved *silently* up the stairs'. Work with your partner and write down words that can replace *silently* in the first sentence of the text to describe all the different ways someone can walk. Use a thesaurus/dictionary to help you.

loudly, _____

3.2 a) Now write down all the words the writer uses to describe the **condition of the room**:

small, _____

b) Work with your partner and write down as many other words as you can that you could use to describe the condition of this room and the furniture. Look at the examples to help you.

Room: *dirty,* _____

Furniture: *shabby,* _____

3.3 The writer lets the reader know that the woman is looking for or expecting something/someone. Write down the parts of the text where the writer suggests this.

_____

_____

Organisation

4 Narratives in stories are organised in different ways by different writers. However, they usually give readers information about the **characters** (the people in the story); the **setting** (place, time); the **events** (things that happened); the **outcome** (what happened in the end). Now complete this grid for the text in exercise 1.

SETTING	CHARACTERS	EVENTS	OUTCOME

5 Although this story has an **outcome** – the woman finds the man – it is not a very satisfactory one. The reader still wants more information. What questions do you think the reader wants answered? Write them here.

_____

_____

_____

6 a) The text below finishes the story started in exercise 1. Read it carefully and find out whether the questions you wrote down in exercise 5 are answered.

b) There is something important wrong with the text. What is it?

> Talbot stared out at me, a thin nervous smile on his lips. So . . . here I am he mumbled. What are you going to do now? I looked back at him in amazement. How different he was! His hair was grey and his skin was pale and wrinkled. His filthy clothes hung from his skinny body. I'm going to do what I've been waiting to do for three years I whispered calmly. I raised the gun slowly until it pointed towards his chest. His lips parted slightly and a flicker of fear passed across his eyes. No . . . not that . . . you have to listen . . . But I was finished with listening. My search was over. The sound of the bullet leaving the gun shattered the silence and echoed in the empty room. He slumped to the floor gasping for air. In the distance I heard a dog bark. I turned away and walked out of the room.

Writing task: Writing dialogue

7 The problem with the text in exercise 6 is that the punctuation and layout of the **dialogue** is incorrect. Look at this piece of dialogue.

quotation marks at the beginning and end of the speaker's **actual** words

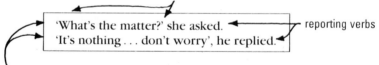

'What's the matter?' she asked.
'It's nothing . . . don't worry', he replied.

reporting verbs

new line for each change of speaker

Now rewrite the text so that it is correctly punctuated and laid out.

Writing task

8 The writer of the narrative in exercise 1 chose to write from the point of view of the **woman**. We 'see' the room through her eyes. Now rewrite the story through the eyes of the **man**. Make the man the 'I' in the story. Imagine that he hears someone coming up the stairs and hides in the wardrobe; when the woman comes into the room he can see her through the keyhole of the wardrobe door. He is terrified that she will find him. He knows her. Her name is Jean.

Remember!
- Write about **events** in the past tense
- Use the past tense of the verb 'to be' to write **descriptions**
- Organise the paragraphs as follows:
  - Paragraph 1: from the time the man first hears the woman until she enters the room
  - Paragraph 2: the woman enters the room, crosses to the window and looks out
  - Paragraph 3: the woman hears a noise from the wardrobe, walks towards it and opens the door
- Use appropriate words to describe the **sounds** you can hear and to describe the woman's movements
- Only write about what the **man** is thinking and can see

Begin like this:

Suddenly I heard the sound of footsteps on the stairs . . .

After writing

9 a) Work with the **Improving Your Writing** checklist in Unit 1. Try to improve what you have written.
b) Exchange texts with your partner. Compare his/her text with the checklist. Can it be improved?
c) Compare your text with the key text on page 78.

Extension activity

10 Now try writing a story of your own. Choose one of the pictures below and, working with your partner, plan a story around it. You will have to imagine what happened before the situation in each picture as well as what happened after. Think about the pictures in terms of **setting, characters, events** and **outcome**. Imagine you are one of the characters in the picture you choose and write from that character's point of view.

A

B

Writing Letters: Expressing Opinions

Discussion

1 When people disagree with something that is happening in their society or want to support a particular idea, they will sometimes start a **campaign**. A campaign is an organised way of working for something you believe in.

1.1 Campaigns start for a variety of reasons. With a partner, make a list of five problems or policies that have caused campaigns (of protest or support) in your country or countries.

Example: Whaling

1. _____
2. _____
3. _____
4. _____
5. _____

1.2 How successful have these campaigns been? Choose one of the problems on your list where a campaign was successful and write a list of two or three things that the campaigners did in order to get what they wanted. When you have made your list use it to tell a partner what happened during the campaign and why you think it was a success.

Example: Stop buying whale meat products

1. _____
2. _____
3. _____

Preparing for writing

2 In Britain there have often been protests about factories that local people believe to be dangerous. The newspaper article below is typical of the sort of problem that people face in many small communities.

Wessex Gazette, May 10th 1988

Anger over armaments factory extension

Residents in the Wessex village of Dornington were furious today as a result of a Ministry of Defence decision to extend an explosives factory where there have already been two serious accidents during the last three years. Residents held a protest meeting in the village hall and a campaign against the proposed expansion was launched by local councillor Mary Loughlin.

2.1 One way of letting people know your opinion is by writing letters. In Britain it is very important to write to your Member of Parliament, the minister responsible for taking decisions and to the newspapers or other interested organisations. The letter below is a good example of this sort of letter. It was written to protest against the factory extension.

The writer of the letter below has organised her writing so that it will get her opinion across as effectively as possible. After you have read it, match the following section labels against the sections in the letter.

☐ ADDRESS OF SENDER   ☐ JUSTIFICATION FOR COMPLAINT

☐ ADDRESS OF RECEIVER   ☐ SIGNATURE

☐ CLOSING   ☐ REASON FOR WRITING

☐ PROBLEM/COMPLAINT   ☐ REQUEST FOR ACTION

☐ DATE   ☐ SALUTATION

☐ FINISHING STATEMENT

```
                                        24, Agnes Street,
                                        Dornington
                                        Wessex                    [1]
                                        WX2 5PU

        May 17th, 1988                                            [2]

        Rt Hon James Dewar
        Minister for Defence
        Ministry of Defence                                      [3]
        Main Building
        Whitehall
        London SW1

        Dear Sir,                                                [4]

        I am writing to you because of possible changes at the MOD    [5]
        factory at Dornington in Wessex.

        We have heard from recent reports that you propose to allow the
        factory here to expand. This will lead to a considerable increase  [6]
        in explosives production at Dornington. We feel that it is unfair
        to impose such a large danger on our community.

        There are two main reasons for our fear:                 [7]

        1. There have been two serious accidents at the Dornington
           factory in the last two years. In one, three workers from our
           village were killed and others badly injured. In the other an
           area of 10 square kilometres was polluted with chemical waste.
           There has never been a public enquiry into these accidents.

        2. We have heard that the planned extension will be for the
           production of even more dangerous materials.

        Because of these very real fears the whole village of Dornington
        has come together to defend itself against your department's
        proposals. We shall fight any plan to expand MOD Dornington
        until your department has agreed to hold a full public enquiry    [8]
        into the accidents at the factory. We also demand that the
        plans for expansion are made public and inspected by an
        independent expert.

        We hope that you understand how worried we are by the changes you
        want to make at Dornington and look forward to hearing from you   [9]
        soon.

        Yours faithfully                                         [10]

        Mary Loughlin                                            [11]
        Councillor Mary Loughlin
```

3 Adjectives and nouns often go together as pairs. Work with a partner to match the nouns in the box with the adjectives in the grid. Then think of a new noun of your own which goes with each of the adjectives. The first one has been done for you.

> accidents changes enquiry expert fears
> increase material reasons reports

a)	considerable	*increase* *interest*	f)	dangerous	
b)	independent		g)	main	
c)	possible		h)	public	
d)	real		i)	recent	
e)	serious				

4 Wessex Gazette, May 18th 1988

Village fury after third explosion

Villagers in Dornington were horrified today when they heard the sound of yet another explosion at the nearby MOD factory.

A spokesman for the MOD said: 'So far we are not sure what caused the explosion. One production worker has been killed and serious damage has been done to the factory's roof. All manufacturing has been stopped for the moment.

Councillor Mary Loughlin – a leading opponent to planned expansion at the factory – told our reporter that the villagers would continue with their campaign against the MOD plans for Dornington. 'We won't let them turn this place into another Chernobyl,' she said.

4.1 Mary Loughlin wrote a letter to the Minister after this new accident. Here are the notes she used:

> 1. accident 18 May completely <u>unacceptable</u>
>   3rd accident 2 years
>   now 4 dead
>
> 2. demand
>   a) immediate close factory
>   b) full public enquiry accident
>   c) public enquiry into future of factory
>
> 3. no more deaths in Dornington
>
> 4. must understand how serious situation - act immediately

Use these notes and the vocabulary lists from Section 3 to write Mary Loughlin's second letter to the Ministry. The letter outline below will help you organise your writing. Let the Minister know that you are very angry about the situation – but remain polite.

- Address of sender
- Date
- Address of receiver
- Salutation
- Reason for writing
- Problem/complaint

- Justification for complaint
- Request for action
- Finishing statement
- Closing
- Signature

4.2 When you have written your letter, first check it against the **Improving Your Writing** checklist in Unit 1. Then exchange your work with a partner and see if you can improve their writing while they work on yours. Discuss any improvements you want to make with your partner before you go on.

4.3 Compare your letter with the key text on page 78 and make any final alterations you think are necessary.

Extension activities

Either

5.1 You live in a quiet part of town and are very happy there until a restaurant starts to leave large amounts of rubbish in the street outside your front door. You talk to the restaurant owner but he refuses to stop so you feel you must write to the Local Environmental Health officer, Ms Jean Archer. You will need the information in the box below.

```
Ms Jean Archer                      17, St Anne's Lane
Environmental Health Officer        Burley
Civic Hall                          Leeds
Leeds                               LS24 3KF
LS1 4UP


Pacific Cafe                           | dustbin
18, St Anne's Lane                     | rubbish
Burley                                 | health hazard
Leeds                                  | warning
LS24 4KF                               | object
                                       | request
                                       | refuse (vb)
```

The letter outline you worked with in the earlier parts of this unit will be very important when you write this. Try to plan your writing so that your argument is clearly and effectively presented.

or

5.2 Work with a partner and write a letter that might have been used during one of the campaigns you discussed in Section 1. Use the letter outline you have worked with during this unit and plan your letter carefully.

After you have written your letter give it to another pair of students. They will now have to write a reply, trying to answer as many problems as they can.

Writing Dialogue

Discussion

1.1 Many different jobs depend on interviewing skills. Work with a partner and write at least four jobs where interviewing is important.

_____

_____

_____

_____

1.2 If you wrote for a magazine, which famous person would you be interested in interviewing? DO NOT WRITE THEIR NAME DOWN OR TELL ANY ONE YET! Write three questions you would like to ask this person on a piece of paper.

Now work with a partner and pretend they are the person you want to interview. Ask them your questions and see if they can guess who you are interviewing. When they have worked it out, try to guess their person.

Preparing for writing

2 Read the following article, which appeared in a local paper in 1988. In order to collect the information she needed for her article, the reporter (Claire Buchanan) had to interview Mrs McFee. Read the article below.

Raiders who today broke into the sub post office run by Mrs Jenny McFee were prevented from taking anything by the bravery of this 64-year-old ex-teacher and her dog, Charley.

Mrs McFee told our reporter that the two young men came into her shop at about 4.30. She was counting the money that she had taken during the day and completing her records of the official payments that had been made through the office, when one of the men pointed a shot gun at her. Mrs McFee followed post office regulations, which say that you should not risk your own safety in the case of armed robbery, and started to give the men some packets of ten pound notes. However, her dog, sensing that something was wrong, came from behind the counter and bit the man with the gun on the leg.

During the confusion Mrs McFee was able to press the switch for the alarm system and lie down on the floor behind the counter. Once the men heard the alarm they panicked and ran off with Charley in pursuit. They were arrested by a police patrol as they tried to escape in their car.

Preparing to write

3 When you are writing dialogue it is important to lay out your work neatly and clearly. Organise the following statements and questions into a sensible order and match them against the correct speakers – either the reporter, Claire Buchanan, or Jenny McFee. Notice how useful it is to leave a space between the speaker and the things they say, and the use of the colon.

Interview: Part one

- Did you think they looked suspicious?
- No. Not at all. They just looked like ordinary boys.
- What did they look like?
- Quite ordinary. One of them wore a brown leather jacket – I think they call them bomber jackets. The other was wearing a T-shirt and jeans. He was carrying a bag.
- The sort of thing they keep sports kit in. It had Adidas written on the outside.
- What sort of bag was that?
- Well, I was counting my takings for the day when I saw these two young men come in. I thought maybe they wanted some cigarettes.
- When did you realise that there was something unusual?

Reporter: Mrs McFee, I wonder if you could tell me what happened first of all?

Mrs McFee:

Reporter:

Mrs McFee:

Reporter:

Mrs McFee:

Reporter:

Mrs McFee:

Reporter:

Focus on language: Contractions in speech

4 When you write words that people say it is very common in English to use **contractions**. It is important to remember that these contractions are only used in fairly informal writing or where you are *quoting* the exact words that someone has used. Two of the main types of contraction in writing are **personal pronoun + auxiliary verb** (eg. *he is*: *he's*) and **auxiliary verb** + *not* (eg. *people could not*: *people couldn't*).

Complete the table of examples given below using the appropriate contractions.

PERSONAL PRONOUN + AUXILIARY VERB		AUXILIARY VERB + NOT	
I am . . .	I'm	we are not . . .	
I have . . .		she did not . . .	
you will . . .		they could not . . .	
she is/has . . .		it is not . . .	
you would/had . . .		I shall not . . .	
it is/has . . .		we cannot . . .	
we are . . .			
they have . . .			

Writing task	**5** Work with a partner and rewrite the second part of Claire's interview with Mrs McFee using **contractions** in all the places where it would be appropriate (there are *eight* places where a contraction should be used).

Interview: Part two

Reporter: When did you realise that there was something unusual?

Mrs McFee: When he pointed that horrible gun at me. I could not believe it at first. I said to myself: 'Jenny, this is not true.' But it was. He started shouting at me: 'Give us the money. Do not try anything or I will blow your head off.' It was terrifying.

Reporter: That must have been awful! What happened next?

Mrs McFee: It is Charley who was the hero.

Reporter: Who is Charley?

Mrs McFee: My dog. He is a black poodle and as brave as a lion. He noticed something was wrong.

Writing task: questions	**6** In order to get information from people you often need to use questions which begin with a question word (*who, what, when, why,* etc.).

Work with a partner to finish the dialogue between Claire and Mrs McFee by trying to write good questions for the answers that Mrs McFee gave. Use *wh-*questions wherever possible. |

Interview: Part three

Mrs McFee: My dog. He's a black poodle and as brave as a lion. He noticed something was wrong.

Reporter: ¹_____

Mrs McFee: As I was giving the money to the man with the gun, Charley came from behind the counter and went straight for him. He bit him in the leg and the man couldn't shake him off.

Reporter: ²_____

Mrs McFee: I think it was because he couldn't stand anyone shouting at me. He just heard this awful shouting and went for the man.

Reporter: ³_____

Mrs McFee: I lay down on the floor behind the counter the moment the man stopped pointing his gun at me. That was when I pushed the alarm button.

Reporter: ⁴_____

Mrs McFee: Oh yes! The moment they heard the alarm they ran for the door. Charley let go of the man's leg and went after them barking as loudly as he could!

Reporter:	⁵_____
Mrs McFee:	Almost straight away. They were really kind. A young policeman got me a cup of tea while a detective asked me questions like you've been doing.
Reporter:	Well, I won't ask you any more now. But thank you very much for giving so much of your time.
Mrs McFee:	Just make sure you get a picture of Charley!

Writing task

7.1 The incident described in this article actually happened! Read the article, then write a dialogue in which the newspaper reporter is interviewing Robert Tolley, the man who ate the frog.

7.2 Once you have written the dialogue and checked it against the **Improving Your Writing** checklist in Unit 1, and against the key text on page 79, work with a partner and practise the dialogue so that it can be performed to a group of people in your class.

> Speaking in his capacity as Secretary of the Hollensworthy Football Club, Mr John White said that his members were very angry about the 1 – 0 result. There had been no score and the match had only a few minutes to run. Then the Hollensworthy team's captain, Jack Tait, spotted a frog hopping across the pitch and asked for play to be stopped while he moved it. Robert Tolley, the other team's captain, came over, picked up the frog and simply popped it into his mouth and swallowed it.
>
> In the amazement that followed Tolley kicked the ball into the goal and as a result his side won the match.

Extension activity

8 Find other newspaper articles (in your first language or in English) and then write similar dialogues using the information and ideas that you find. Remember to lay the dialogue out clearly and when your class has written three or four, arrange a performance of the ones that are the most interesting or amusing.

Writing Persuasively

Discussion

1 Are you influenced by a book's cover when you are buying it or borrowing it from a library? There is an English proverb that says: 'You can't tell a book by its cover', but we can all be persuaded to buy a book by the things on its jacket as well as by the writing inside.

1.1 Work with a partner and find out about three books (fiction or nonfiction) that they have read or used recently. What did they pay most attention to when they were choosing the book?

Give a score out of five for importance of the following things (5 = very important, 0 = completely unimportant). Compare your two results with the results of the rest of your class and decide what makes people buy or borrow books.

THE BOOK'S AUTHOR	
REVIEWS YOU HAVE READ	
COVER PICTURE	
THE PUBLISHER	
WRITING ON THE COVER	
RECOMMENDATIONS FROM FRIENDS	
PAPER QUALITY	

Focus on language

2.1 The following extracts come from different parts of three books – the introduction and the writing on the cover (this is often called the 'blurb'). Work with a partner and decide which extracts are from the cover and which are from the introduction. Mark the text I or C.

A. **Read *Chinese Vegetable and Vegetarian Cooking* and you will never think of vegetables as dull again. Go one further and try some of the recipes.** ☐

B. Of the six novels Forster wrote, *A Room with a View* had the longest period of development. ☐

C. Cooking and serving a Chinese meal, vegetarian or otherwise, presents some different problems from serving or cooking a western one, since a Chinese meal is usually communal. ☐

D. The present book is to some extent based on the *Complete Book of Card Games* (written in collaboration with my friend B.C. Westall) which first appeared in 1939. ☐

E. In this brilliant piece of social comedy Forster is concerned with one of his favourite themes. ☐

F. *The Pan Book of Card Games* – Fifty card games and twenty-eight games of Patience. Outstanding – no other book of card games explains so many games so thoroughly or offers so much instruction. ☐

2.2 When you recognised the cover extracts in the last exercise you noticed certain words and phrases in the passages that showed you the writer was trying to **persuade** us to read or buy the book.

> In this <u>brilliant piece of social comedy</u> Forster is concerned with one of his favourite themes.

2.3 Work with a partner and mark any words or phrases in the other two book cover extracts that you think are being used to make the writing persuasive. Compare the words you have chosen with other pairs. Do they have many things in common?

2.4 Features

The writing on the book covers needs to be persuasive. It describes the special **features** of the books that will attract a reader and (especially in non fiction) it describes the **benefits** the book might give to the reader.

In this complete extract from the blurb for Kenneth Lo's cookery book the features have been <u>underlined</u>.

Kenneth Lo

Read *Chinese Vegetable and Vegetarian Cooking* and you will never think of vegetables as dull again. Go one further and try some of the recipes. <u>No special expertise is needed, the methods of preparation and cooking are explained step by step and no previous knowledge of Chinese cooking is required.</u>

Kenneth Lo, well known expert on Chinese food, makes it all so straightforward. The book is <u>arranged according to method of cooking</u>, so that you can quickly master stir-frying, for example, and can try the many recipes which can be made in this way before going on to another method. There are also <u>sections on sauces, soups, rice, pasta, eggs, bean-curd, hot and cold salads and sweets</u>.

Notice how the **features** of the book often contain lists of the special qualities of the book – the things that make it different from other books in the market. The other sections of the blurb often refer to the reader as 'you'. These sections tell the reader about the **benefits** the book can give them.

2.5 Verb forms

What verb forms have been used in these four extracts from the blurb.

A. | **Read *Chinese Vegetable and Vegetarian Cooking* . . .**
    Go one further and try some of the recipes . . .

INTERROGATIVE ☐ IMPERATIVE ☐ PASSIVE ☐

B. | **The methods of preparation and cooking are explained step by step . . .**
    The book is arranged according to method of cooking . . .

INTERROGATIVE ☐ IMPERATIVE ☐ PASSIVE ☐

2.6 Verbs to use

Now read this blurb from the back cover of the *Longman Active Study Dictionary*. The special features of the book are clearly described. However, there are other parts of the text that talk directly to the reader.

Underline the sections where the reader is talked to directly and write the main verb that was used in each statement. The first one has been done for you.

Longman Active Study Dictionary of English

– the new learning dictionary for intermediate English students that <u>helps you to speak, write and read English</u>.

▶ **38,000 words and phrases**

▶ **55,000 helpful examples**

▶ **Clear accurate definitions** using the Longman defining vocabulary of 2000 common words

NEW
▶ **Study Notes**
   – clear, full-page guides to grammar and major language points
   – you can use them to learn by yourself or teachers can use them in class

NEW
▶ **Workbook Introduction**
   – exercises to give you practice in using the dictionary

▶ **Usage Notes**
   – to help you avoid common mistakes in English

▶ **Phrasal Verbs**
   – new layout to show correct positions of objects

▶ **IPA pronunciation guides**
   – full coverage of British and American English

▶ **Easy-to-use grammar information**

---

a) helps _____

b) _____

c) _____

d) _____

(Note that sometimes it is quite difficult to decide whether something is a feature or a benefit; they may be both.)

2.7 Sounding certain

a) When you write persuasively it is important to be **certain** about what you are saying. Underline the words in the two sentences below that tell us about the writer's attitude:

1. The new *Vegetarian Gourmet* may be useful for some people . . . ☐

2. *The Meat-Lover's Handbook* is a book that will please all its readers . . . ☐

Which sentence sounds more certain, 1. or 2.? Put a tick beside the one you choose.

b) The words in the box on the left will make statements sound more or less certain. Work with a partner to sort them into two different columns – **more certain** and **less certain.**

sometimes	very	will
all	always	certainly
quite	rarely	should
must	nearly	never
many	may	might
completely	every	is

MORE CERTAIN

LESS CERTAIN

Improving your writing

3 The piece of writing for a book jacket that is given below is not as **persuasive** as it should be. Work with a partner to improve it. You will need to pay particular attention to how **certain** the writing is. It will be necessary to remove or change many words before the writing is really persuasive.

> ## The best travellers language companion (*Russian Edition*)
>
> If you buy this book you might have a more enjoyable holiday.
>
> This nearly completely revised new edition should help a traveller make him or herself understood in quite a lot of situations in Russia. The book has:
>
> - a dictionary section that helps many people look up words and phrases
>
> - quick reply features – just point at a phrase written in Russian and sometimes people might give you an answer in English
>
> - pronunciation – this is shown in most parts in the book and may help you be understood more easily by some of the people you talk to

Writing task

4.1 Planning your writing

Look at the notes below about a new book called *The Blue Guide to Britain.* The notes give a very detailed account of the **features** of this guide book. They do not say anything about the **benefits** the book will give to the person who buys it.

BLUE GUIDE TO BRITAIN	
Easy to use format; includes following details:	• Cities – cinemas, theatres, museums, leisure centres, restaurants

Maps
• Regional routes
  – motorways and minor roads
• Street plans of Manchester, Leeds, London,
  Birmingham, Edinburgh, Glasgow. Cardiff,
  Belfast, Bristol, Cambridge, Oxford
	General information
	• Food, history, traditions, industry,
	  national holidays
	• Art galleries, concert halls, hotels,
	  campsites, accomodation, leisure parks

Attractions
• Regional – national parks, historic sites
  (castles, cathedrals, great houses)
	Useful information
	• Addresses and telephone numbers
	• National and international transport
	  facilities
	• Money

Work in a group of three or four and brainstorm the possible benefits of the book. Once you have this list, select and write down the most important and interesting points from the notes and the list your group has made.

Example: You can find your way around anywhere from London to Glasgow.

4.2 Now use the ideas above to help you write the back cover blurb. You can use up to 150 words, but no more, so you should not try to include *all* the information you have. Be as persuasive as you can; you think the book really is useful!

4.3 After you have written the text, exchange your writing with a partner and see if you need to change or add anything. Check your work against the **Improving Your Writing** checklist and finally compare it with the key text on page 80. Do you think it would be really persuasive?

Extension activity

5.1 Choose a book that is well known either in your country or internationally and try to write a blurb for this book. Do not *name* the book when you write about it. Exchange your writing with other people in your group after you have checked it yourself to make it as good as possible, and see if they can guess the book's title.

Writing a Composition: Saying What You Think

Discussion

1 In examinations and many other settings you are often asked to give your opinion in writing. In this unit you will be writing a short composition in which you will have to say what you think about a particular topic. To begin with, work in a group to find out other people's ideas about this question:

'Meat eating is as bad for you as it is for animals.'
What is your opinion?

1.1 Brainstorming
A good way to begin writing an essay is to make lists of ideas that you can select from later on. Work in a group of three or four to make a list of all the ideas you have about meat eating. Write a list of reasons why you think it could be good to eat meat and list of reasons why you think it may be bad.

REASONS FOR
Protein, balanced diet,

REASONS AGAINST
Cruel, wasteful of land,

1.2 Does your list contain more good things than bad things? Make a total for each of these and compare your ideas with the ideas of other groups. Do people in your class think that meat eating is good or bad for people.

GOOD	*BAD*

Model text

2 The short composition below is an example of a very common way of organising a piece of writing where you have to give your opinion. Read the essay carefully and then work with a partner to use the section labels in the box and name the different parts of the composition.

| JUSTIFICATION | PROBLEM | OPINION |
| FINAL COMMENT | BACKGROUND INFORMATION | |

'Meat eating is as bad for you as it is for animals.'
What is your opinion?

Human beings have eaten meat for many thousands of years. We have teeth that can cut and chew meat and stomachs that can digest meat. In many parts of the world it is the main food of most people and perhaps it always will be. However, during this century there have been many changes in the way animals are looked after and

| 1 |
| 2 |

the way meat is produced. Now, there are many people who think that meat eating is not good for you.

| 3 |

I agree with these people. In my opinion, the changes in the way meat is produced have been so serious that I do not want to buy meat or eat meat. For example, chicken has become a very popular food in Britain in the last twenty years. In the past it was quite expensive and you ate roast chicken on Sunday or on special occasions. Now it is very cheap and people can eat it every day, but it is not as good as it was. This is because the chickens are kept in very bad conditions in very small spaces and they are fed with hormones and antibiotics to keep them healthy until they are killed. Not only are the chickens killed in a horrible way after a horrible life, but I think the meat from these chickens is not good for you. It is full of water (to make it heavier) and chemicals and it does not taste good. I do not feel that this sort of meat is good for me and I am happier eating vegetarian food which is cheaper and tastes better.

| 4 |

Perhaps the statement 'Meat eating is as bad for you as it is for animals' is too extreme. I do not think that people should all stop eating meat immediately or that meat will kill you. However, I do not think that meat is very good for you any more and I do not want to eat it myself.

| 5 |

(328 words)

Preparing for writing

3 A composition where you have to give your opinion about a particular topic can be organised like the model text above and will have the same sections. These are not always in separate paragraphs, but they are usually in this order.
When you plan your composition you should have ideas for each of these sections.

> 1 BACKGROUND INFORMATION   2 PROBLEM
> 3 OPINION   4 JUSTIFICATION   5 FINAL COMMENT

3.1 Background information
In this section you give background information that will help the reader understand the **topic** you are going to write about and the **context** you are writing in. Reread this section of the model text and copy the grammatical subject of each sentence into the box below.

> Human beings have eaten meat for many thousands of years. We have teeth that can cut and chew meat and stomachs that can digest meat. In many parts of the world it is the main food of most people and perhaps it always will be.

a) [ ]   b) [ ]   c) [ ]

It is important to notice that you often start your writing by describing the situation without talking about *your* opinion. That often comes a little later in the composition.

3.2 Writing task: PROBLEM

a) It is very common to introduce the PROBLEM section of a composition with a **contrast** marker. Read the next section of the model text and write the word or words that show contrast between the ideas of the BACKGROUND INFORMATION and the ideas of the PROBLEM.

> However, during this century there have been many changes in the way animals are looked after and the way meat is produced. Now, there are many people who think that meat eating is not good for you.

b) Use these **contrast markers** to connect the sentences given below.

1. When the motor car was invented everyone thought it would give easy, cheap transport to the people of the world.

2. The car has created problems as well as making life easier for many people.

3. Life is more difficult in many cities because of this helpful invention.

3.3 Writing task: OPINION

The writer of the model text thought that eating meat was bad for you. Rewrite the OPINION section of the model text to say that eating meat is a *good* thing and that you want to go on eating meat. This is what the writer said.

Old version:

> I agree with these people. In my opinion, these changes have been so serious that I do not want to buy meat or eat meat. . .

You can use some of the phrases below in your writing:

- In my opinion . . .
- I think that . . .
- I feel that . . .
- I agree with . . .
- I disagree with . . .
- I object to . . .

New version: _____

_____

_____

3.4 Writing task: JUSTIFICATION

The JUSTIFICATION section of your composition is often the longest part. In it you must give reasons that support your opinion.

Work with a partner and use these notes to complete a justification section for the composition about meat. This writer thinks that meat is good for you.

> 1. e.g. Meat a very important food (protein)
>   not enough meat can lead to MALNUTRITION
>   many vegetarians not have good diet - even in rich countries
>   most important give children + manual workers enough meat
>   (grow / be strong)
> 2. CHANGES in farming methods = good for all people.
> 3. Now meat very clean + safe - killed carefully and stored
>   better today than past (refrigerators)
>   In past meat = food rich people
>   NOW meat low price - so everyone has enough
>   People taller, stronger, healthier
>   Meat always be important food for human beings

3.5 Writing task: FINAL COMMENT

In the FINAL COMMENT section it is very important to say clearly what your opinion is and to connect it with the title of the composition. You always need to be able to make this connection.

Use the model text as a guide and write a FINAL COMMENT section for this essay from the point of view of someone who thinks it is **good** to eat meat. Begin this section as follows:

The statement 'Meat eating is as bad for you as it is for animals' is too extreme and untrue . . .

Writing task

4 You should now be able to write your own composition. Use the title:

'Television has always had a bad influence on society.'
What is your opinion?

4.1 Start your writing by thinking of answers to the following questions.

- When was television invented?
- What percentage of countries in the world have television systems?
- What proportion of families that you know do not have televisions?

4.2 Make a list of all the ideas you have about the effect of TV on modern society. Write down good things and bad things.

GOOD THINGS?	BAD THINGS?
Education, entertainment,	Violence, political control,

4.3 Look back at the model text, exercise 2. Using the same writing sections, write a composition of around 300 words.

4.4 Improving your writing

After you have written your composition you should read it through yourself, using the **Improving Your Writing** checklist in Unit 1. Pay particular attention to the information you have put into your composition and make sure you have organised it appropriately.

4.5 Ask a partner to check it through for grammar, spelling and punctuation errors. Then check your writing with the key text on page 80.

Extension activity

5 Write a second composition that uses the same type of planning.

'Men always make better managers than women'.
What is your opinion?

Work in the same way as in this unit. Brainstorm some ideas and organise them into a writing pattern similar to the one you have just used.

Answer key

UNIT 1   Improving Your Writing

1.1 Suggested answer:

CORRECT GRAMMAR	
APPROPRIATE VOCABULARY	
GOOD SPELLING	
CLEAR ORGANISATION	✓
CLEAR, APPROPRIATE LAYOUT	✓

1.3 1 L: date under your address
　　 2 L: county after the town
　　 3 ST: in a formal but friendly letter, begin *Dear Mr/Ms Smith . . .*
　　 4 G
　　 5 G: adverb, not adjective
　　 6 SP
　　 7 G
　　 8 ST: use *because* in more formal writing
　　 9 V
　　10 V
　　11 SP
　　12 V: we just say *repair*
　　13 ST: you need to use a politeness marker, e.g. *I would be grateful if . . .*
　　14 ST: you need a **closing** phrase like *Yours sincerely,*

3.1 Our company makes glue and glucose and is also involved in the grain business. It is 130 years old and has different sections in various parts of the country.
　　　　Our production centre is in Wodenswil, the main grain business is in Samstagern and we have big stores in Olten and Au. We also have a small water-mill (although this is not very important for the company) and we have about 200 employees.
　　　　The organisation of the company is quite simple. It buys wheat, maize and barley from overseas suppliers and from some local farmers and has eight vans that it uses to deliver glue and glucose to its customers. We don't do a lot of advertising for our products and only advertise in local newspapers.
　　　　The only problems that the firm has are that it is rather dependent on the value of the dollar and that sometimes there is too much work to do. At such times our workers are seriously overloaded, but they receive extra payments during these periods and the company continues to do well.

3.2 He opened the door to the library, stepped in and looked towards the tables where *people* sat studying and *shut* the door carefully behind him.
　　　　He was a man of middle height, *dressed* in a blue coat which looked a bit *old-fashioned*, but still *suited* him well. He was in his twenties, had a hard-looking face with dark eyes and thick eyebrows. His hair was brown and short.
　　　　As he walked through the library he looked around him as if *searching* for somebody. When he *noticed* the person he was looking for his severe expression disappeared and was *replaced* by a warm smile.

3.3 Are factories spoiling our rivers?
Nowadays *many* factories are very irresponsible. Not only do they use *a great deal of* clean water but they poison the rivers with their chemicals. Moreover, since *they have failed to clean* the rivers the water system is *becoming more and more polluted*. Therefore, we cannot swim and drink any water *from* the rivers. In addition, *fish from the rivers cannot* be eaten. As a result, fish is very expensive.
　　There was a *problem* in Japan a long time ago. A lot of people who ate the fish *became* ill. This was because the fish had a disease.
　　In conclusion, we can say it is dangerous to *dump* filthy water into rivers.

3.4 I think one of the best *ways* to learn a language is to stay and *live* in the country where it is spoken because then *you have* to speak in every situation in this language. You have to try *to make yourself understood,* so you can *learn the language* in a short time. You *do not have to study for such a long time as you do* when you take an evening course every evening in your own country.

UNIT 2   Organising Your Writing Using Linking Words and Phrases

1 d, a, f, e, b, h, c, g

2 The next day, Then, this time, first, then, When, the following day, by now, then

3 1 First of all 2 then 3 Later 4 As 5 By 6 before 7 eventually

4.1 a) Just as (same) b) while (same) c) until (before)/in the meantime (before) d) then (after)/Finally (after) e) by the time (before)

4.2 a) While b) before c) When/After d) As/Just as e) then

5 Similar to *and:* also, in addition, also
Similar to *but:* Although, However

6 Dear John,
I arrived in England last Saturday and my course began on Monday. I'm living about three kilometres from the school but it only takes me about fifteen minutes to get in every morning by bus.
　　Everyone at the school seems very friendly and there are two other French students in my class. However, I don't speak French with them during the day because we all want to practise our English as much as possible. The course is good and the social programme is quite interesting as well. I feel I have a good chance of passing the exam in June although it is only three months away.

7 1 and 2 but 3 because 4 After 5 although 6 so

8.1 The woman gave the boy a small box. He took it from her and put it on the ground. He opened it. Inside the box was a package. He opened it.

8.2 old lady with the green hat, George, her, she, She, a baby, she, he, her, George, the poor woman

8.3 a) **Wants to help the woman:**
Man: kind, pleasant, honest-looking, gentle, friendly, young man, youth
Woman: elderly, friendly, amiable, genial, cheerful
Wants to harm the woman:
Man: evil-looking, scruffy, filthy, dirty, aggressive, suspicious
Woman: poor, frail, wretched, fragile, vulnerable, frightened, terrified
b) Suggested answer:
A poor, frail old woman was standing by the side of the road waiting to cross. Suddenly, a scruffy, evil-looking teenager came along and grinned unpleasantly at her. The filthy swine grabbed her arm and reached over to take something from her bag.

UNIT 3 Writing a Journal

1.2 **Student A** thinks regular tests are good. Wants to do tests at home and go over problems in class.
Student B likes the 'fast reading' computer program and thinks it really does help her to improve her reading speed.
Student C thinks watching videos is useful but wants them to be replayed several times. Also thinks listening to songs is useful.

2 a) Examples: (A) We had a test. (B) We did a practise in fast reading in the computer room.
b) Examples: (A) Today we did what I always wished to do. (B) I like the program of fast reading.
c) Examples: (A) Tests are important to show you where you still are weak. (B) I think it is because I read a lot. (C) It makes me very happy when suddenly I can understand the whole meaning of a song.
d) Examples: (A) Why can't we make such an exercise in class? Why not work with a sheet at home and ask questions at school?

3 2) Describing something that happened in the classroom
3) Giving reasons
4) Making suggestions

4.1 a) We use the **past tense** to describe things that happened in the classroom.
b) We *had/studied/watched* a video; We *did/had* a test; We *practised* answering exam questions; We *did/had/studied/ practised* some grammar exercises; We *studied/did/had* a reading passage.

4.2 a) **Feelings**: bored, interested, excited, tired, pleased, enthusiastic
Qualities: exciting, boring, dull, interesting, tiring
b) **Examples**:
i) . . . it helps you to understand the structure of the language.
ii) . . . you get more opportunities to speak.
iii) . . . I feel embarrassed.
c) Yesterday we interviewed some people in the park. In my opinion it was useful because it gave us the chance to speak to ordinary people.

4.3 Examples:
a) I think we should spend more time looking at grammatical problems.
b) I'd like to have regular vocabulary tests.
c) Why don't we do more work on listening skills?

6 KEY TEXT Suggested answers:
Day 2: Today we interviewed some people in the street. It was very interesting but I found it quite frightening because I was embarrassed about speaking English. However, it was good to talk to English people outside the classroom. I think we should spend more time practising the questions we are going to ask before we go out.
Day 3: Today we wrote an essay. It's useful to practise writing essays but I found it very difficult because there was not enough guidance from the teacher. I'd like to have more guidance in future.
Day 4: Today we had a test. Tests are very useful because they allow you to know something about your strengths and weaknesses. Why don't we have a test every week?

UNIT 4 Writing a Postcard

1 b) A Applicant to potential employer B Bank manager to account holder C Boyfriend to girlfriend D Friend to friend E Employer to employee F Boyfriend to girlfriend

2 Description of a place: C and F
Description of the weather: C
Expression of feelings: C and F
Arrangements for the future: C
Description of things that have happened: F

3.1 a) Size: huge, enormous, large, big, immense, vast, small
Location: isolated, exposed, hidden, sheltered
Atmosphere: calm, tranquil, restful, busy, lively
b) We're staying in a small, pretty hotel at the foot of a mountain, which is covered in snow. The hotel is quite isolated and surrounded by pine trees. Everything is so peaceful.

3.2 Postcard C: fantastic
Positive: beautiful, amazing, fantastic, wonderful
Negative: dreadful, awful, terrible, lousy, freezing, dull, miserable, rotten
Neutral: OK, quite warm, not too bad
Positive or Negative depending on your view: sunny, hot, cool

3.3 Postcard C: 'Having a lovely time'.

3.4 Dear John, Having a lovely time. Went to visit a monastery yesterday – had to climb 400 steps up the side of a mountain! Look forward to seeing you on my return. Best wishes, Sally

3.5 a) Suggested answer:
We went south yesterday to visit a castle on the Rhine. The weather was terribly hot and humid, but fortunately there was plenty to drink on the boat! The castle was in a beautiful location, perched high on a cliff overlooking the river. We enjoyed the trip very much.

b) Suggested answer:
We took a boat up the river yesterday. Although we were in Disneyland it really did feel like being in the jungle! The sun was hot and we passed groups of elephants playing in the river and spraying each other (and our boat!) with water.

3.6 Close relative, boy/girl friend: Lots of love, All my love, Love, Best wishes, See you soon, All the best
Acquaintance: Regards, See you soon, Best wishes, Yours, All the best

4 Suggested order: 2, 3, 6, 4, 5, 1

6 KEY TEXT Suggested answer:
Dear Pam, Having a lovely time. The weather's great – although it's very hot, there's almost no humidity. I'm staying in a small hotel on the edge of the desert. Yesterday I visited a Bedouin Family and stayed to lunch. Everyone was very kind and hospitable. See you when I get back. Love John.

UNIT 5   Writing Small Ads

1 a) 2 b) 1 and 9 c) 6 d) 8 e) 3

2 a) pcm b) Tel. c) pw d) eves. e) CH f) incl.
g) excl. h) mod. cons. i) vgc j) lge

3 a) For Sale. Amstrad 1640 computer, vgc, £350 ono.
b) Accommodation available. Room in lge house. £120 pcm incl. CH. Tel 63421 eves.

4 b) Professional male, 40, cheerful, seeks female companion. Must be easy-going. Letter to Box 412
c) Room wanted near city centre. Single male, 25, professional, non-smoker. Tel. 46312 (eves).

5 Suggested answer:

ACCOMMODATION TO LET

Small room available in flat, Baker Street.
£40 pw, CH. Tel: 635–7129 eves.
Total number of words: 13
Total cost: £2.60

6.1 a) These are adverts from people looking for friendship.
b) Advert D
c) Advert G (*widower* means a man whose wife has died)
d) The writers of adverts D and E could be introduced to each other. They are around the same age, are both educated and enjoy the theatre, music and outdoor activities. He is from Newcastle and she mentions Newcastle in her ad.
The writers of adverts D and C could also be introduced to each other for similar reasons.
The writers of adverts G and E might also get on well. They are close to each other in age, both have (probably) been married before, both are educated and both enjoy theatre, music and outdoor activities.

6.2 Warm attractive female. . . seeks romantic, unattached, humorous male, 38–50. Photo/phone appreciated. Box 4888.

7 Personality: charming, humorous, easy-going, caring, cheerful, kind, generous, reserved, mad, genuine, nice

Appearance: attractive, slim, medium-build, nice, glamorous
Education/Job: intelligent, educated, professional, successful

9 KEY TEXT Suggested answer:
Male graduate, 25, just moved to Colchester, easy-going, enjoys theatre, films, music, sports, seeks similar female friend to help him get to know the town. Letter please. Box 3456.

UNIT 6   Writing a Letter of Thanks

1 a) A: applicant/potential employer B: nephew/uncle and aunt C: friends D: ex-student/teacher
b) A: for sending an application form B: for a gift C: for letting her stay D: for help in passing the exam
c) Letters B and D are similar in important ways (see exercise 2).

2 a) Thank you very much . . . /It's just what I need!/thanks to your present . . ./Thanks also for the lovely card.
b) No – it's too short and sounds rather rude.
c) Paragraphs 2 and 3 are included for politeness only. Without them, no **information** would be missing but it would be **impolite.**
d) **Paragraph 1:** Say thank you for the first time
Paragraph 2: Explain how the gift will be useful
Paragraph 3: Ask about health
Paragraph 4: Say thank you again

3.1 a) Thank you very much for the money you sent me for my twenty-first birthday.
b) Thank you very much for the book you gave me for Christmas.

3.2 a) Examples: fantastic, magnificent, marvellous, gorgeous

6 KEY TEXT Suggested answer:

> 77 Vestergade
> Aarhus
>
> 25 March 1988
>
> Dear Mr and Mrs Abbot,
>
> Thank you very much for the money you sent me as a wedding present. I was so surprised to receive it and am very grateful.
> We are about to move into a new house and as we have no cutlery or crockery, your gift will be most useful!
> I hope you are both well and that we will meet again soon.
> Thanks also for the beautiful card.
>
> Yours sincerely,
>
> Birgit Hansen

UNIT 7   Writing Telegrams and Telex Messages

1.2

> **Telegram:** A piece of paper with a message sent by telegraph (by radio or electrical signals along a wire. . .)

> **Telex:** a message sent from one teleprinter to another by telephone line

(We are grateful to Longman Group UK Ltd for permission to use extracts from the Longman Dictionary of Comtemporary English, pub. 1987.)

2.1

Tientsin Airport
People's Republic of China

15.4.88

Janet Evans
Impex Group
17 Great Portland St
London. NW1

Dear Janet,

I have been delayed at the airport and I will not arrive in London until 17.54 on Saturday evening. Could you please tell Michael what is happening?

Perhaps we could meet at lunchtime on Sunday at my hotel. The address is:

Hotel Albermale,
24 Wilton St.
London NW1
(Tel 01-487-5892)

My apologies for the inconvenience,

Yours sincerely,

Katarina Belsdorf

2.2 Prepositions: in, at
Personal pronouns: you, my
Auxiliary verbs: have, could
Articles: the

3 Information: Delayed airport. Arrive London 17.54 Saturday.
Request for action: Please tell Michael . . . etc.

4

> 16.4.88
>
> BELSDORF. NEW CHINA HOTEL. TIENTSIN. PRC
>
> WILL SEND CAR TO MEET YOU AT AIRPORT. HAVE TOLD MICHAEL. OK MEET SUNDAY. BEST WISHES.
>
> JANET

5

> 17.4.88
>
> EVANS. IMPEX GROUP. 17 GREAT PORTLAND ST. LONDON NW1
>
> PLANE DELAYED 24 HOURS. WILL COME LONDON MONDAY 6.40 AM. POSSIBLE SEND CAR AIRPORT. PLEASE TELL MICHAEL BRING DOCUMENTS YOUR OFFICE. MEETING IMPEX MONDAY AFTERNOON. APOLOGIES.
>
> KATARINA

6.2 KEY TEXT Suggested answer:

> Subject DELAY IN DELIVERY OF ORDER 3462
>
> REGRET CANNOT DELIVER BEFORE 20.8.88 LORRY STRIKE IN ATHENS. IMPOSSIBLE FIND OTHER COMPANY.
>
> MANY APOLOGIES.
>
> MARIA

UNIT **8**   Writing Short Narratives: A Fable

2 2; 4; 3; 1

2.1

3	Later events	2	Earlier events
1	Setting the scene	4	Describing the final outcome

2.2 a) *One day,* a Hare was making fun of a Tortoise . . .
b) *Once* there was a farmer who was working on his farm when . . .
c) *Long ago* there was a king who loved gold . . .
d) *There was a time* when all the animals could talk . . .

2.3 A crow was sitting on the branch of a tree with a piece of cheese in *her* mouth when a hungry fox saw *her* and started to think of how *he* could get the cheese for *himself*.

3 Once upon a time the Sun and the North Wind had an argument over who was the strongest. The North Wind said, 'I am stronger than anything. I can blow *over* the tallest tree and take the roofs *off* all the houses!' In order to discover the truth they agreed to test their strength *on* a traveller. They would see who would be the first to take his coat *from/off* his back.   `Setting the scene`

The North Wind was the first to try. He gathered all his force and began to blow as hard as he could. However, the harder the wind blew, the tighter the man held on to his coat, so that in the end the North Wind was so exhausted he had to give up.   `Describing earlier events`

When the Sun began, all he had to do was to shine brighter *in* the sky. At first the man undid the buttons of his coat. Then, as the sun's warmth increased, the man took *off* his coat and carried it over his arm. He was very happy to walk along like this, feeling pleased *at* the change *in* the weather.   `Describing later events`

The North Wind was very angry and went off behind the hills, but the Sun rose higher and higher *in* the sky. 'Don't you know that persuasion is better than force!' he said.   `Describing the final outcome`

75

4.1 A1   B5   C4   D3   E 6   F 2

5.2 KEY TEXT Suggested answer:
Once there was a boy who looked after his village's sheep. He thought it would be a good joke to frighten everyone by pretending that a wolf was attacking the sheep.

He ran down into the village shouting 'Wolf! Wolf!' All the villagers ran to the fields where the sheep were but there was no wolf to be seen. The boy laughed but the villagers did not think it was funny. The boy played the same trick several times and the people of the village always came to help him. However, they did not like his tricks at all.

One day, a wolf really did come to the field where the boy looked after the sheep. He ran to the village crying 'Wolf!' as loudly as he could. The villagers told him to go away. They did not believe him now. He asked them to come many times but they told him to go and play his tricks on someone else.

Because of the boy's lies many sheep in the field were killed and he was beaten by his father. The boy learned that you cannot believe a liar even if they are telling the truth.

UNIT *9*   Writing a Report: Describing Graphs

2 Factors affecting population growth: medical care, availability of food, attitudes to family size, contraception, death rates amongst children and adults
Aims of population control programmes: reduce child mortality by making better medical care available, make family planning information and services accessible, encourage the idea of small families

3 The part of the graph that is missing relates to Latin America. The figure for 1950–55 is 2.7%, and the figure for 1995–2000 is 2.2%

4.1 Paragraph 1: The overall picture of world population growth
Paragraph 2: Details of changes in a particular region
Paragraph 3: Details of changes in a particular region

4.2 Sentence 1: General comment on whole period for a named area
Sentence 2: Details of changes during each time period
Sentence 3: Expectations for the future

4.3 a) G   b) P   c) P   d) G   e) P   f) G

5.1 a) declined, reached, reducing, fell, continue to fall, dropped, plummeted
b) **Upward:** increase, rise, grow, soar, leap, rocket, shoot up
  Downward: decrease, plummet, decline, drop, slump, dive

5.2 a) slightly, dramatically, significantly
b) i) The rate increased sharply in the 1960s.
   ii) The rate fell slightly in the 1970s.
   iii) The rate leaped suddenly in 1940.
c) **Small:** gradual, slight, moderate, steady
  Large: sudden, rapid, dramatic, great
   i) slight
   ii) sudden/rapid/dramatic/great
   iii) steady/gradual
   iv) moderate
   v) dramatic/great/sudden/rapid

7 KEY TEXT Suggested answers:
Africa is the only region of the world where the rate of population growth has increased sharply over the period covered by the graph. The rate shot up from just below 2.2% in the early fifties to 2.7% in the late seventies and reached a record high of 3% in the eighties. It is hoped that the rate will come down slightly over the next ten years, to a projected level of 2.9% by the year 2000.

Europe has the lowest rate of population growth in the world, and it has decreased steadily over the period covered by the graph. After a slight increase from just under 0.8% in the early fifties to a peak of 0.9% in the sixties, the rate fell to 0.7% in the early seventies and then plummeted to around 0.4% during the late seventies and eighties. It is expected that the rate will be around 0.3% by the year 2000.

UNIT *10*   Writing in Newspapers

2.1 Article 1
● Trapped under his car for . . .
● 'I broke my arm when . . .
● That was why I hit . . .

Article 2
● Asked why he had decided . . .
● 'I was lying down waiting . . .
● 'As they struggled with each other . . .

3 Article 3: Interviewed at her mother's house in Tokyo, Mrs Shano Urati said:

Article 4: Interviewed outside his place of work, Mr John Topton, a counter clerk at Barclay's Bank, Snairwell, said:

4 My husband worried about losing his hair. A street-doctor convinced him that the only certain way to cure his baldness was to fast. After accepting this advice he ate nothing for 40 days and on the 41st he died. His hair had shown no signs of returning.

5 Interviewed outside his place of work, Mr John Topton, a counter clerk at Barclay's Bank, Snairwell, said:
'We were busy at lunchtime and there was a long queue. All at once a man came under the rail, stuck a gun over the counter and demanded the money in my cash drawer. I was about to follow the manager's instructions to hand over some money and press the alarm bell, when Mr Bobby Grove, a customer who was waiting to be served, came up behind the man, grabbed him and, shouting "Queue jumper!", marched him out of the bank and into the street. It was quite a relief.'

6.3 KEY TEXT Suggested answer:
Reporting on the results of Operation Good Driving, in which the French police decided to give cash prizes to the good and careful drivers they observed, Minister of Transport, M. Pierre Mehaingerie, said: 'The operation was an absolute failure. The motorway patrols could find no good, careful drivers. One quite good driver was seen, but he increased his speed to 140 kph and drove into the thickest traffic. They couldn't find anyone wearing a seat-belt or keeping within the speed limit.
'Finally they found a man who they thought could get a prize when, for no reason at all, he went straight past three red traffic lights. The driver must now pay a large fine instead of receiving the 500 francs prize.'

UNIT 11 Writing a Speech

1 b) Include: welcome the guests; give details of her career and experience; welcome and express gratitude to the speaker; refer to the length of the talk; introduce the speaker by name and refer to the general subject of the talk; introduce the particular topic and relate her experience to it

2 1: welcome guests 2: introduce Dr Tomlinson and general topic of talk 3: refer to her career 4: introduce hijacking and her experience in this area 5: thank Dr Tomlinson for coming 6: refer to length of talk and questions

3.1 (1.4) . . . a topic she knows a great deal about; (1.5) . . . her highly successful career; (1s.9–10) . . . the first woman ambassador; (1.11) . . . an expert; (1s.12–13) . . . she has been directly involved; (1.18) . . . long experience

3.2 a) delighted, proud, honoured
b) a topic she is very knowlegeable about; an area in which she has great expertise
c) Suggested answer:
I am delighted to introduce our speaker for this evening, Mr Clark, who is going to talk to us about international finance, an area in which he has considerable expertise.

4.1 a) began, (working), worked, took up, remained, moved, became, occupies, is, is, has been . . . involved, will concentrate, (resolving)
b) Verbs that refer to a particular time in the past: began, worked, took up, remained, moved, became.
Verbs that refer to the past but not to a particular time: has been involved
Verbs that describe her qualities and interests: occupies, is, is
Verbs that refer to the coming talk: will concentrate

5 Suggested answer:
Mr Clark began his highly successful career in the International Section of the Bank of England in 1973. In 1977 he became the youngest person ever to be a director of a merchant bank. After joining the World Bank in 1983, he became Vice-President in 1987.

Mr Clark is an expert on the funding of international projects, and a particular interest of his is agricultural projects. He has been directly involved in large irrigation projects in Sri Lanka, China and Egypt.

7 KEY TEXT Suggested answer:
Good evening ladies and gentlemen. Thank you all for coming. I am delighted to welcome our speaker for this evening, Ms Yvonne George, who is going to talk to us about the care of the mentally disabled.

Ms George began her career in 1974 when she joined Camden Social Services as a social worker. In 1979 she became a Member of Parliament and six years later was made Minister for Health and Social Security.

She is very familiar with the problems of the mentally disabled and has been closely involved in a number of recent schemes for integrating the mentally disabled into the community.

I'd like to take this opportunity to thank you, Ms George, for giving up your precious time to come and speak to us tonight to give us the benefit of your many years experience of dealing with this issue.

I understand Ms George is going to speak for about forty-five minutes, and there will be about fifteen minutes left for your questions and comments. So, would you please welcome tonight's speaker, Ms Yvonne George.

UNIT 12 Writing Narratives: Telling a Story

2 a) 1 at the door (looking in) 2 at the door (inside) 3 at the window 4 at the wardrobe
b) The paragraphs in this text are associated with the woman's position in the room. In paragraph 1 she is outside the door looking in. In paragraph 2 she has moved into the room and closed the door. In paragraph 3 she is at the window and in paragraph 4 at the wardrobe.

3.1 a) silently, noiselessly, quiet, empty, scraping sound, quietly
b) Examples: loudly, noisily, slowly, quietly, briskly, clumsily, carefully . . .

3.2 a) small, airless, layer of dust, bare floorboards, old furniture, broken chairs, dirty sofa
b) Room: filthy, dirty, dark, depressing, dismal . . .
Furniture: shabby, damaged, filthy, scruffy, torn, ripped, stained . . .

3.3 'I could feel that I was getting close' (the writer tells us she is looking for someone); 'and there *he* was' (the writer tells us she has found what she was looking for)

4 Setting: an upstairs room somewhere
Characters: a man and a woman who know each other
Events: woman comes up the stairs and into the room; she looks around and walks to the window; she hears a noise and walks to the wardrobe; she opens the wardrobe door
Outcome: she finds the man

5 Examples: Who is the man? Who is the woman? Why is the man in this room? How did the woman find him? Why is the woman looking for him? What is she going to do next?

6 b) Punctuation and layout is inappropriate.

7 Talbot stared out at me, a thin nervous smile on his lips.
'So . . . here I am', he mumbled, 'What are you going to do now?'
I looked back at him in amazement. How different he was! His hair was grey and his skin was pale and wrinkled. His filthy clothes hung from his skinny body.
'I'm going to do what I've been waiting to do for three years', I whispered calmly.
I raised the gun slowly until it pointed towards his chest. His lips parted slightly and a flicker of fear passed across his eyes.
'No . . . not that . . . you have to listen!'
But I was finished with listening. My search was over.
The sound of the bullet leaving the gun shattered the silence and echoed in the empty room. He slumped to the floor, gasping for air. In the disance I heard a dog bark. I turned away and walked out of the room.

9 KEY TEXT Suggested answer:

Suddenly I heard the sound of footsteps on the stairs. Could it be her? I ran to the wardrobe and closed the door behind me. The door handle turned and someone entered the room. My heart began to pound.

There was silence for a moment. Then the footsteps started again. I peered through the crack in the door. It was her! She had found me! My legs began to shake uncontrollably as I watched her cross to the window. She stopped again and looked out.

As I moved to get a better look at her my foot stumbled against something on the bottom of the wardrobe. I cursed inwardly. She was facing me now and moving purposefully towards the wardrobe. Suddenly she flung the door open . . .

UNIT 13   Writing Letters: Expressing Opinions

1.1 Suggested answers:
1. Whaling	4. Nuclear weapons
2. Fur trade	5. Abortion
3. Acid rain	

1.2 Suggested answer: Whaling
1. advertising in newspapers/cinema/TV
2. writing to MPs and governments
3. direct action against whaling ships

2.1

ADDRESS OF SENDER	1
ADDRESS OF RECEIVER	3
CLOSING	10
PROBLEM/COMPLAINT	6
DATE	2
FINISHING STATEMENT	9
JUSTIFICATION FOR COMPLAINT	7
SIGNATURE	11
REASON FOR WRITING	5
REQUEST FOR ACTION	8
SALUTATION	4

3 Suggested answers:

a) **considerable** increase interest
b) **independent** expert advice
c) **possible** changes advantages
d) **real** fears difficulty
e) **serious** accidents concern
f) **dangerous** materials activity
g) **main** reasons purpose
h) **public** enquiry outcry reports difficulties
i) **recent**

4.3 KEY TEXT Suggested answer:

> 24, Agnes Street
> Dornington
> Wessex
> WX2 5PU

May 20th, 1988

Rt Hon James Dewar
Minister for Defence
Ministry of Defence
Main Building
Whitehall
London SW1

Dear Sir,

I am writing to your department for a second time as a result of the explosion that happened at the MOD factory in Dornington on May 18.

This explosion is completely unacceptable. It is the third accident in two years and now four people have died.

We demand that you close the factory at Dornington immediately, order a full public enquiry into the accident and allow a public enquiry into the future of the factory. There must be no more deaths in Dornington!

I hope that you understand how serious the situation is and that you act immediately.

Yours faithfully,

M. Loughlin

UNIT 14   Writing Dialogue

1.1 Examples: doctor
journalist
TV/radio presenter
opinion pollster

3 Reporter: Mrs McFee, I wonder if you could tell me what happened first of all?

Mrs McFee: Well, I was counting my takings for the day when I saw these two young men come in. I thought maybe they wanted some cigarettes.

Reporter: What did they look like?

Mrs McFee: Quite ordinary. One of them wore a brown leather jacket – I think they call them bomber jackets. The other was wearing a T-shirt and jeans. He was carrying a bag.

Reporter: What sort of bag was that?

Mrs McFee: The sort of thing they keep sports kit in. It had Adidas written on the outside.

Reporter: Did you think they looked suspicious?

Mrs McFee: No. Not at all. They just looked like ordinary boys.

Reporter: When did you realise that there was something unusual?

4

personal pronoun + auxiliary verb	auxiliary verb + not
I am . . . I'm	we are not . . . we aren't
I have . . . I've	she did not . . . she didn't
you will . . . you'll	they could not . . . they couldn't
she is/has . . . she's	it is not . . . it isn't
you would/had . . . you'd	I shall not . . . I shan't
it is/has . . . it's	we cannot . . . we can't
we are . . . we're	
they have . . . they've	

5 Mrs McFee: When he pointed that horrible gun at me. I *couldn't* believe it at first. I said to myself: 'Jenny, this *isn't* true.' But it was. He started shouting at me: 'Give us the money. *Don't* try anything or *I'll* blow your head off.' It was terrifying.

Reporter: That *must've* been awful! What happened next?

Mrs McFee: *It's* Charley who was the hero.

Reporter: *Who's* Charley?

Mrs McFee: My dog. *He's* a black poodle and as brave as a lion. He noticed something was wrong.

6 Reporter: [1] What did he do?
Reporter: [2] Why do you think he did it?
Reporter: [3] What did you do then?
Reporter: [4] And did the men run out straight away?
Reporter: [5] When did the police come?

7.2 KEY TEXT Suggested answer:

Reporter: Mr Tolley, I'd be grateful if I could have a few words with you.

Robert Tolley: Well?

Reporter: It's about this business with the frog. Could you explain for our readers what happened out there on the field?

Robert Tolley: Look. Our team had been having a hard time all through the match. Hollensworthy had blocked our game and we hadn't had a chance to score. I was really angry by the time Tait asked the referee to stop the game.

Reporter: Exactly why did he do that?

Robert Tolley: Because there was this frog. Tait saw it in the middle of the field and called the referee over. He wanted to have time to pick it up and carry it off the field so it wouldn't be trodden on.

Reporter: And what did you do?

Robert Tolley: I picked it up and ate it. I was really angry, I just wanted our team to have a chance to score and win the match. We were in a good position when Tait called to the referee and I didn't want to miss the chance.

Reporter: What happened then?

Robert Tolley: I just got on with the game. There was no frog and so there was no reason to stop. I ran with the ball and got the winning goal. I don't see what all the fuss is about myself!

Reporter: And what did the frog taste like?

Robert Tolley: I don't know really. It was only small and I didn't chew it. It slipped down and I didn't taste anything, I suppose.

UNIT 15 Writing Persuasively

2.1 A. C D. I
B. I E. C
C. I F. C

2.5 A. **Imperative:** You can use *imperatives* when you are telling people to do something that will be **good** for them.
B. **Passive:** You often use the *passive* when it is unimportant to mention **who** has done something.

2.6 a) helps c) give
b) use d) help
When you are writing persuasively it is very common to use verbs like this. They show how the book will be useful for the reader.

2.7 a) 1. The new 'Vegetarian Gourmet' *may* be useful for *some* people. . .
2. 'The Meat-lover's Handbook' *is* a book that *will* please all its readers. . .
Sentence 2: sounds more certain
b) **More certain:** all, always, certainly, completely, every, must, never, very, will, is
Less certain: many, may, might, nearly, quite, rarely, should, sometimes

3 THE BEST TRAVELLERS LANGUAGE COMPANION (Russian Edition)

Buy this book and you will have a more enjoyable holiday.

This completely revised new edition will help you make yourself understood in every situation in Russia. The book has:

● a dictionary to help you look up words and phrases

● quick reply features – just point at a phrase written in Russian and people will give you an answer in English

● pronunciation – this is shown in all parts of the book and will help you be understood more easily by everyone you talk to

4.3 KEY TEXT Suggested answer:

THE BLUE GUIDE TO BRITAIN

You need never be lost again! *The Blue Guide* gives you all the information you will ever need about this fascinating, varied country. In its easy-to-use format you will find:

Maps:
that show you not only towns and roads, but regional information on national parks and historic sites

Street plans:
of major cities in the UK, plus details of cinemas, theatres, museums and restaurants – now you can find your way around anywhere from London to Glasgow

General information:
on the culture and traditions of Britain, as well as guides to entertainment and accommodation throughout the country – you need never be stuck for something to do with *The Blue Guide*

Useful information:
including addresses and telephone numbers, advice on money and national and international transport facilities –*The Blue Guide* has everything you need for your holiday, and will even help you get home afterwards

UNIT *16*   Writing a Composition: Saying What You Think

2 1 BACKGROUND INFORMATION
2 PROBLEM
3 OPINION
4 JUSTIFICATION
5 FINAL COMMENT

3.1 a) Human beings   b) We   c) it

3.2 a) However; Now
b) When the motor car was invented everyone thought it would give easy, cheap transport to the people of the world. *However,* the car has created problems as well as making life easier for many people. *Now* life is more difficult in many cities because of this helpful invention.

3.3 I do not agree with these people. I feel that these changes have not been too serious and I do not want to stop buying or eating meat.

3.4 Meat is a very important food for all of us and is our main source of protein; not enough meat can lead to malnutrition. Many vegetarians do not have a good enough diet even in the rich countries and it is most important that children and manual workers have enough meat in order to grow and be strong. Changes in farming have been good for all of us. The meat that we eat is now much cleaner and safer than in the past; it is killed carefully and stored better too. In the past meat was a food for rich people but now meat is low priced so everyone can have enough and we are taller, stronger and healthier than ever before. I think that meat will always be important food for human beings.

3.5 The statement 'Meat eating is as bad for you as it is for animals' is too extreme and untrue. I do not think that people should stop eating meat. In fact, I think that we should produce more meat for more people so that all human beings can have the chance of growing healthier and stronger. I feel that meat is good for you and I shall certainly keep on eating it.

4.5 KEY TEXT Suggested answer:
'Television has always had a bad influence on society'. What is your opinion?

During the twentieth century television has been one of the most important influences on society. Television exists in nearly every country in the world and can be seen even in the poorest societies. In industrial societies such as Britain, over 95% of households have televisions. Television is a strong influence. Is it always for the good?

In my opinion television has probably had a bad effect on society as a whole. I feel this is the case for three main reasons. Firstly, television has always received its money from advertising or governments. This has meant that it can never be free of the influence of very powerful groups who have strong reasons for maintaining the present organisation and power structure of society. Secondly, television programmes are very expensive to produce and broadcast. Because this is the case it is always necessary to have as large an audience as possible and, unfortunately, a large audience is more interested in the Eurovision Song Contest or The A-Team than in material that is genuinely educational or challenging. Finally, television is broadcast for too many hours. It stops people thinking and reduces everything to the same level. A disaster in Beirut or Belfast becomes as unreal as murder and death in a fictional programme.

Television is not a bad thing in itself. However, I feel that in its present form it has always been abused, has always taken power away from its audience and has created a violent, materialistic culture that has become dependent on the medium that created it.

(257 words)